Ministry to and with the Elderly

By

Timothy M. Farabaugh

authorHOUSE™

1663 LIBERTY DRIVE, SUITE 200
BLOOMINGTON, INDIANA 47403
(800) 839-8640
WWW.AUTHORHOUSE.COM

First published by AuthorHouse 03/30/05

ISBN: 1-4184-8729-5 (sc)

Printed in the United States of America
Bloomington, Indiana

This book is printed on acid-free paper.

I would like to dedicate this book to my mother and father, who have been a source of inspiration in their ministry to older adults, to my mother- and father-in-law, who have provided encouragement throughout my ministry, and to my wife and children, who have stood beside me throughout my ministry both in the local church and in long-term care settings. The love and support of my wife has enabled me to step outside of the local church and follow my calling to a full-time ministry to the elderly.

Table of Contents

Introduction

Through my experience as a local church pastor and as an administrator in long-term care facilities, I have become aware of the unique needs of the older adults as well as the distinctive contributions they are able to make in the life of the local church. As a result of this experience, I have felt compelled to share some of my insights with those who are called upon to provide pastoral care to the older adults. Through this book, I would like to help local church pastors and seminary students understand that the elderly of our congregations not only have unique needs but also offer extraordinary talents that could greatly benefit others in the congregation. If nothing else, the wisdom garnered from the experiences of a lifetime enable the elderly to serve as advisors to those of us who are struggling with the vast array of decisions that confront us individually and as a congregation of believers. Through many years of struggle, the older members of our congregations have developed and matured physically, emotionally, and spiritually. The task of the pastor is to recognize the gifts as well as the needs of their aging parishioners and to find a way to accept the gifts and meet the needs. Hopefully, this book will serve as a tool to assist the clergy in this task.

Chapter One
What do you mean "Old"?

Age is a matter of mind; if you don't mind, it doesn't matter.

The middle-aged elementary school teacher comes home worn out and complains that she feels "old" after a day of working with ten-year-olds and a host of younger colleagues. To the newly wed couple in their twenties, their parents who celebrate their twenty-fifth wedding anniversary seem old. It's hard for them to imagine that they will ever reach that age. A recent retiree looks at his parents in their eighties as "old." A visitor to an assisted-living facility sees people using walkers and canes and says that she is not ready to go live in a place full of "old folks." The lady in her nineties refers to the lady who is over a hundred as "the older lady."

We have a lot of fun when people reach mileposts in their lives like their fiftieth birthday. Some of my favorite sayings on such occasions may also shed some light on what it means to be "old." You're over the hill when ... you see your old cereal bowl in an antique shop; your arms grow too short to hold your reading material; the barber charges you a finder's fee; you add "God willing" more often to your statements; everyone has already heard all your stories; you feel most comfortable driving five miles under the speed limit and straddling two lanes; you resign yourself to the fact that certain foods are not compatible with your gastrointestinal system; sometimes you stop to think and forget to start again; you can't remember when you didn't eat prunes and bran flakes for breakfast; you pursue members of the opposite sex and forget why.

What is "old"? Who is "old"? The answer depends, oftentimes, on the age of the person asking the question. To the six-year-old, it may be anyone over ten. To the teenager, it may be anyone over twenty-five. Old means different things to different people. The American Association of Retired Persons offers membership to adults who are fifty years old and over. The Bureau of Census defines those between the ages of sixty-five and seventy-four as "elderly." Those people who are between seventy-five and eighty-four years of age are placed in the "aged" category. And those people who are eighty-five years old and older are defined as "very old."

For our purposes, I would prefer to define the older adult as one who is older than age sixty-five. My rationale is that age sixty-five is the normal retirement age in the United States. Most of our cultural rites of passage are associated with this age. Retirement catapults those who reach it into a new era. No longer are they compelled to get up and go to a job for eight hours a day. As a result, daily routines change, one's identity changes, relationships with one's spouse and co-workers change, and one's income changes.

These statistics will help us better define the elderly as well as the opportunity the church will have to minister to and with this age group in the years to come. In 1970 there were 203,982,310 people in the

United States. Of that number, 20,097,490 were over the age of sixty-five. Of the people who were more than sixty-five, 1,430,010 were eighty-five years old or older. In the year 2000, the population of the United States was 274,758,390. Of that number, 34,410,000 were over the age of sixty-five, and 4,054,000 were eighty-five years old or older. The number who were older than sixty-five nearly doubled between 1970 and 2000. Those who are more than eighty-five will nearly tripled! By 2030, the estimated number of people over the age of sixty-five will be close to 70,000,000.[1]

In the early part of the twentieth century, the average life expectancy was about fifty years. The life expectancy in 1990 was about seventy-five years. Part of the reason for this increase in our life expectancy is the tremendous strides that have been made in the field of medicine over the past century. We are able to do so much to prevent illness and to cure illnesses when they do occur. A second reason our life expectancy has increased by nearly twenty-five years has been better nutrition. We are keenly aware of our nutritional needs and have provided good support in programs like school lunches for our children and Meals on Wheels for our seniors. The final reason for increased longevity is better sanitation. Indoor plumbing, underground sewage, and sewage treatment plants have helped to keep infections under check and drinking water pure.

The implications of this situation are quite clear. Lower mortality and longer life expectancy mean that for the first time in human history, a society will exist

---

[1]   U.S. Census Bureau

wherein most of its members live to be "old." This is good news for those who are aging, but we have, by virtue of this fact, created other problems. The United States Congress has, for several sessions, been struggling to decide how to ensure that Social Security will remain solvent once the "baby boomers" are in need of its benefits. Funds for Medicaid and Medicare will have to be increased in order to be able to meet the growing needs of the elderly. The typical "sandwich generation" children, who once were working and in their forties or fifties when it came time to care for their parents, are now closer to retirement age themselves, living on incomes that are substantially lower than they once were. Our ministry to the elderly will continue to grow and our ministry to their children will increase as well. The churches that used to be catering to young adults and children will be forced to take a hard look at what they must do for the elderly.

Richard Gentzler, Jr., D.Min., who works at the office of adult ministries with the United Methodist Church, published a catalog of resources for churches ministering to the elderly. In the introduction, Dr. Gentzler says that "In the United Methodist Church today, approximately 62% of its membership is 50 years and older."[2] An article by Pamela Stone found in the *Interpreter* magazine indicates that 25 percent of the United Methodists are age sixty-five or older. I would imagine that if I were to check with other denominations, the statistic would be similar. We are

---

[2]   Richard H. Gentzler, Jr., D.Min., *1999 International Year of Older Persons* (Nashville, United Methodist Publishing House: 1998), 1.

an aging nation, and as a result an aging church. These statistics must compel us to ask ourselves "What does this mean to us in terms of our ministry for the future?" and furthermore, "What changes will we be required to make to meet these new demands?" Any denomination, any congregation, regardless of its religious affiliation, will be faced with these same questions.

Ministry to the older adult encompasses all the "normal" kinds of pastoral care. Home visits, hospital visits, and nursing home visits are the kinds of pastoral care that we normally think of for this age group, but there is much more we can do to assist the older church member. From the issue of loss that is felt upon retirement, to the loss of a spouse, to the loss of home, we find circumstances that can produce stress, create depression, and test faith. Aging voices of choir members, loss of hearing, and crippling arthritis affect the ability of the elderly to participate fully in worship and church social activities. Poor eyesight and impaired judgment make it difficult and indeed dangerous for the aging church member to come to worship. After sixty or seventy years of church attendance, there is a feeling of loss or even of abandonment on the part of the elderly who can no longer attend worship. In addition to these needs, the older church members see the truth of one's finality every day. Friends they have known for years die. Their own mortality becomes quite clear. These older people need the love and attention of their minister and their church family. In the future, the need for this sort of pastoral care and attention will increase as our population continues to age.

I had an older parishioner tell me when I asked how she was doing, "Well, okay I guess. I read the paper this morning and didn't see my name in the obituary column." The humor of this statement points to the fact that death is something the elderly are faced with daily. The unique need theologically is to work out their belief about life after death and to prepare for it. Existential anxiety cripples those who are not sure what their future holds. Pastors and fellow Christians have the unique responsibility of helping the elderly talk about these concerns and helping them develop a faith strong enough to enable the older church member to live out his or her days with assurance and hope. As the number of post-retirement years continues to expand, so do the opportunities to think about life and its meaning. The nearness and certainty of death compels the older adult to contemplate more often and in greater detail the meaning of life and the possibility of life beyond this one.

Although many of the pastoral needs of the elderly are just like the needs of the younger congregation members, there are many other pastoral needs that are unique to the elderly. They require the clergy to be aware of and attentive to these needs as they attempt to minister to the elderly.

When we think about the over-sixty-five age group, it is obvious that there are a variety of needs based upon age and situation, but I would suggest that one of the fundamental pastoral needs is assistance to the elderly who suffer from both role and status attrition. It seems that the post-retirement age group faces similar problems in at least three areas. The first common area is the loss of roles that come with retirement, which excludes the aged from significant social participation and in effect devalues them. There are very few exceptions to the normal retirement age. With work come an identity and a sense of self-worth. As a result of retirement, the older person becomes marginal and alienated from the larger society. They tend to be tolerated, ignored, rejected, and seen as a liability. The second common area is that in old age people find themselves in the first stage of life with systematic status loss for an entire cohort. Every phase before retirement is marked with social growth and advancement. With old age, people who were highly valued for both their performance and their achievements are suddenly redefined as old and obsolete. The real problem here is that the elderly person does not understand this new image he has acquired. For years all had gone well. He had not done anything wrong. He was not a failure. His only crime was his age. The third area where pastoral care is necessary is in the realization that our society is not socialized to the fate of aging. During each stage of life we are prepared for the next, but not so with old age. The expectations for old age are not well defined, and because there is no blueprint or job description we can hardly prepare for it. The competitive society in which we live does not prepare us to fail or lose status. The church must be prepared to assist those who find themselves in a change of role as individuals and by virtue of being "old," and to assist the elderly as they live while preparing to die.

I am sure that we can provide pastoral care to the elderly. We have been doing it for years. In the coming generations, we will simply have to focus more of our attention and energies on meeting these needs. The area where the church is most lacking is in its understanding of how the elderly can be involved in ministry. We naturally think of the many ways our older members need pastoral care, but we do not often think of how they can help provide pastoral care. Who knows better than he or she who has had to adjust to loss of identity through retirement, the feelings of those going through this traumatic time? It makes good sense for us to use the laity who have struggled through the issues we associate with aging to assist those who currently face them.

One of the mottos of the AARP is "To serve, not to be served." I believe that those who are just past retirement are able to provide any number of services for their church including pastoral ones. They are also a good source of volunteers in other capacities. As the elderly age, their physical limitations may prohibit them from performing the strenuous work, but they may still be of great service to others. No one wants to be a burden. Most everyone wants to feel useful. It behooves the church to find opportunities for the older member to be in service to others. If we were to think about it, the truth is that these older adults bring wisdom, tenacity, spiritual depth, and life experiences that are valuable to our churches.

There are many kinds of programs wherein the laity are trained to provide pastoral ministries to those in need. By identifying the unique needs of the elderly as well as those who have similar adversities, it is quite possible to pair up one elderly person with another. They become a support for each other.

In addition to using older adults to help each other, they can also function in many other ways within the life of the church. In any given church you will find people age sixty-five or older serving as church schoolteachers, board members, trustees, ushers, choir members, and much more. The church must continue to use the elderly in whatever capacity they are willing to serve or where their spiritual gifts are of greatest value. But it seems that we should use them most where they have the most to offer. Simply by virtue of age, the older person brings with them experience and wisdom. We should continue to seek their guidance, to enable them to serve in positions where they can be of greatest assistance to individuals and to the church as a whole. In addition, this age group has something very few other adults have: time. They often have more flexible schedules, which give them more time to volunteer at the church. Can you imagine what would happen if one day a week a luncheon was prepared for older adult volunteers who would come to the church building to assist with making follow-up calls to visitors, or sending welcome cards to new neighbors, or typing the bulletin or perhaps folding it, or answering the phone, or leading a Bible study or devotional at noon? The projects are endless. The results may save the church thousands of dollars, and at the same time develop a ministry by the older adult!

I attended a seminar on aging a few years ago where the speaker, Dr. Henry Simmons, the director of the Center on Aging at the Presbyterian School of

Christian Education in Richmond, Virginia, told us that we are the first generation who expects to die of a degenerative rather than an infectious disease. We have taken for granted that our medical knowledge and technology have enabled us to fight infections and win. Now, our demise will come as a result of a worn-out body. With successful heart, lung, kidney, and joint replacement surgery, even some of the parts of our bodies that degenerate are no longer the cause of death or discomfort that they once were. Due to our technological and medical advancements, we are living longer.

Living longer, however, presents some additional problems. Humanness, it seems, is defined in our culture by physical intactness, looking young, and being productive. Many people over age sixty-five lose legs due to diabetes. Many others have had strokes that have left them disabled. Hearing and sight difficulties often set the elderly aside as a person with a deficiency, someone not quite as "good" as the rest of society. The same can be said of gray hair, wrinkles, and a slow gait. In the United States, "young" is ideal. We are so concerned with the physical appearance that we see people who are less than that youthful ideal as not as good, not as worthy of our attention. We also tend to evaluate people's worth on their ability to be productive. "What do you do?" is a question with which we determine if the other person is okay or not. Certain professions are held in higher esteem than others. Certain levels of management or titles are seen as worthy of our praise and admiration. If the person is no longer working, they are seen as less worthy. We make these decisions consciously and unconsciously. They affect how much attention we pay to them and how willing we are to do what is in our power to assist them. We tend to desire to associate with people who are by status a step above ourselves. We join organizations, even churches, to be with the people with whom we like to associate.

Those people who are over age sixty-five are marginalized by society. They are set aside, pushed away. They no longer have power or authority and are treated as if they do not count for much. But the sixty-five-plus age group has had and will continue to have an influence on our national politics. That means it will have an influence on the decisions made regarding health care, retirement, and economic issues. Though most of society treats the older adults as non-productive has-beens, they still wield the sword of the vote, and they do. A greater percentage of those over age sixty-five vote than any other age group.

Another area where the elderly can be influential is in finances. I remember one particular shut-in who always had her church offering envelope waiting for me when I brought her communion. I learned over time that she gave 10 percent of her income to the church. She gave another 10 percent to support a TV evangelist that she watched on Sunday morning. Though I cannot quote figures, I believe I am correct in stating that the elderly give a higher percentage of the income to the church than any other age group. Older adults have already paid the mortgage. Some are no longer driving, avoiding car expenses. Certainly their income is less in retirement than when they worked, but they do not have work-related expenses to consider either. The contributions to the church's ministries made by the elderly can make a positive impact in any congregation. Be sure to offer programs that will benefit them as well as other age groups.

The important thing those in authority must remember is that because someone has retired does not mean they are of no value. Rather than say that they are old and forget about them, we must continue to discern their gifts and talents that can be used to enhance the ministry of the church.

We have a unique opportunity these days to be in ministry to and with an age group that continues to expand from retirement to well beyond one hundred years of age. The needs and abilities of the sixty-five-year-old are not the same as those who are ninety or one hundred. The common thread between them is that they are retired, and in our society that places people in a particular category. Pastors need to be aware of the needs of the older adults as well as their abilities as we attempt to minister to them and to assist them as they minister to others.

Chapter Two
Physical Conditions

Age stiffens the joints but softens the heart.

When we talk about ministry to and with the older adult, it is imperative that we understand some things about that sixty-five-plus age group. In this chapter, I would like to discuss the physical condition of the elderly and some of the medical problems common to this age group. When I talk about an age group that goes from sixty-five to one hundred, it is obvious that not everyone has or will have the conditions listed below, but generally speaking I will explain the most common ailments and diseases that afflict this age group. My intent is to help the reader get a firm grasp of some limits the older adult might have as a result of physical decline and diseases common to the elderly. This knowledge will assist the clergy as they plan to meet the pastoral needs of the older adult.

I would like to begin this topic with an explanation of several theories regarding why and how people age. They can be categorized into one of two general classes. The first class or group of theories is called intrinsic or "biological clock" theories. As the name implies, the belief here is that we are biologically programmed to age the way we do. The programmed theories claim that the aging process is generated intentionally by the organisms from within (intrinsic) by the readout of a program, which is encoded within the DNA of the body's cells. Aging is seen in much the same way as the development and maturation of an individual. It is an extension of the normal developmental process, with some variation produced by interaction with one's environment. The general concept is that a biological clock is located somewhere in the body or in the cells that, at a certain time, turns on or off specific genes leading to age-related changes in the body. Many people place this biological clock with the brain.

The second class of biological theories of aging is called the extrinsic, stochastic, or "wear and tear" theories. These theories compare our bodies to that of a machine. The genes provide the body with a strong and viable physiology at about the time of sexual maturity. Over time, one's physiology degenerates due to normal unavoidable damage to body tissues, as well as abuse we heap upon ourselves. Ultimately, the accumulated damage causes failure of some critical biological system, and death results. In this theory, aging is a passive process, produced by internal and external agents that cause damage to the body's systems.

It is easy to see the validity of both these theories. There are some syndromes that have been identified that give great validity to the "biological clock" theory. The Hutchinson-Gilford syndrome and Werner's syndrome are examples wherein people with these rare genetic mutations are doomed to a short life in which many of the hallmarks of advanced age occur very early in life. Yet these cases are rare, and perhaps the more "normal" aging occurs as our bodies simply wear out over time.

There was a study done by Alexander Leaf, in *Scientific American*, where he compared people who were seventy-five years old with persons who were thirty years old. He found in this study that those who were seventy-five years old had 92 percent of their former brain weight, 84 percent of their former basal metabolism, 70 percent of their former kidney filtration rate, and 43 percent of their former maximum breathing capacity.[3] What he is telling us with these statistics is that, on average, when a person reaches age seventy-five, their brain weighs 10 percent less, their body is burning calories at a reduced rate, their kidneys are filtering about three-fourths as fast, and their lungs process oxygen more slowly. The implications of this information are that there is a slow-down, decrease, or decline in the physical body as it ages.

Generally speaking, though Leaf's data compares people age thirty to those age seventy-five, aging is not a sudden event that happens at a certain age. It is, as one would assume, a gradual, continuous process that begins at birth. We know that at least some of the systems of the body decline at different rates in different individuals. They do, however, decline in all people, from the point of their fullest development to a point where they have lost much of their abilities.

A study done by Kane, Ouslander, and Abrass in 1989 indicates that under normal circumstances, the body rejects foreign cells, but as the body ages, there is a progressive weakening of the immune system. The result of this weakening is that the elderly become more susceptible to respiratory and other illnesses.[4]

[3] Alexander Leaf, "Getting Old," *Scientific American* (1973): 44-53.

[4] R. L. Kane, J. G. Ouslander, and I. B. Abrass, *Essentials of Clinical Geriatrics,* 2nd ed (New York, 1989), 10.

For that reason, the elderly are encouraged to get flu shots each fall and tend to be more careful about colds and traveling, even to worship, in bad weather.

Choosing between these two classes of theories is less important than understanding the differences and being aware that no matter how we age, the fact remains that we do so. We all get old, and as we do our bodies change.

I have listed below a brief synopsis about the more common illnesses found in the elderly. Some of these are found in other age groups as well. In fact, many of the problems the elderly face are due to conditions of an earlier age. When we provide pastoral support to the aged, and especially to those in a nursing home or assisted-living community, we will see more infirmities than during home visits to the elderly. These folks have needs that they can no longer meet on their own. Assistance from nursing professionals is required.

Cardiovascular Disease

Like the immune system mentioned above, which is affected by the aging process, the cardiovascular system is affected too. The degradation of the functional ability of the cardiovascular system usually interferes with the much-needed supply of nutrients and oxygen to the cells. As a result, the tissues and organs of the body are damaged. This damage leads eventually to the decline of other major processes.

As we age, we run a greater risk of cardiovascular diseases. These diseases include a wide range of disorders that may destroy the blood vessels of the heart. The combination of these diseases is the leading cause of death throughout the world. Such things as heredity, poor nutrition, and the environment may influence them.

The circulatory system is made up of two interconnected systems. They both begin at the heart. These systems are called the systemic circulation system and the pulmonary circulation system. In the systemic system, the blood is pumped from the left ventricle of the heart into the aorta. Then the blood moves into smaller and smaller arteries until it comes to the very small capillaries where the blood actually moves through the body tissues. After it flows through this tissue, it starts on its return trip to the heart, being collected by veins until it enters the right atrium.

The pulmonary system circulates the blood from the right ventricle into the pulmonary arteries and through the lung capillaries. It is here in the lung capillaries that the blood picks up the much-needed oxygen and moves by veins back to the heart through the left atrium. Since the capillaries are the areas where the oxygen and foodstuffs go into the body cells and where waste products are removed, any vascular disease is sure to affect in some way the function of the tissues that are supplied by the capillaries.

When we talk about cardiovascular disease, we talk about two major types. The first is artery disease and the second is vein disease. The most significant cause of artery disease is the thickening and hardening of the artery walls by deposits of fatty materials. These deposits may occur as a result of a fatty diet, high blood pressure, or any number of genetic factors.

The second type, vein disease, involves the formation of blood clots. These clots usually form in the legs. The major factors that cause these blood clots are: 1) slowing of the blood stream; 2) the increase of ability of the blood to coagulate; and 3) an injury to the lining of the vein. Clots that form may break off and travel to the right side of the heart. From there, the clot may be pumped to the lung, but it gets trapped as the pulmonary artery gets smaller. Once trapped, the clot may block or restrict the flow of blood to a portion of the lung, creating a pulmonary infarction. The immediate shock may be fatal. We see this kind of problem most often in postoperative hospital patients. Though it seems cruel, it is important that our parishioners, who have just undergone surgery, get up and walk as soon as possible to avoid the possibility of these clots forming in their legs.

Related to cardiovascular disease is heart disease. Most heart diseases are related to insufficient blood supply to the body tissues we talked about above or overwork of the heart muscle. There are two kinds of heart diseases. They are either congenital or acquired. Congenital disorders result from abnormal development of the heart, but acquired disorders are due to heredity, environment, and infectious processes that cause damage to the heart, the arteries, the valves, or the conduction tissue.

The acquired disorders affect the elderly most often. In this case, the coronary arteries become blocked. That results in a lack of blood to the heart. Angina and shortness of breath usually result. If the blood flow to an area of the heart stops completely, heart muscle cells die. The result is what we commonly call a heart attack. The cells that have died form a scar and no longer function as a part of the heart muscle.[5]

Some of the more common risk factors for coronary artery disease are: smoking, elevated cholesterol levels, obesity, hypertension, and diabetes mellitus.

One way we may be able to help the elderly in our churches combat the normal decline we witness in aging cardiovascular systems is to offer a moderate exercise program. An example of this is a senior social program that encourages older adults to remain active through shared meals, bus tours, sports, and volunteering in the childcare center. If the church offers a senior program, chair exercise that encourages movement of arms, legs, heads, and other extremities should be a part of it. Many churches object to dancing in the facility, but a modified line dance for seniors is very popular and serves to increase blood flow and, as a result, oxygen to the necessary organs. There are many activities the elderly can enjoy. Shuffleboard and badminton do not require great physical strength or agility. Men seem to enjoy the physical activities more than women do. Indoor games like ring toss are reminiscent of horse shoes many of them tossed as children and young adults. Most of the older churches I have visited have shuffleboard courts in their social halls. The game seems to have fallen out of favor with

---

[5]   *Grolier Multimedia Encyclopedia,* 1998, s.v. "Cardiovascular."

younger people, but the elderly would still enjoy it. Many hospitals offer an exercise program for those people who have had heart attacks or undergone heart surgery. This often includes walking a certain distance. If you go to nearly any shopping mall before the stores open in the morning, chances are you will run into mall walkers who are able to exercise in a safe, comfortable atmosphere. Could we not open our church social halls for the same purpose? There are videotapes available to guide senior adults through a series of exercises that are not too strenuous yet offer good results. Not only do these kinds of exercises help the elderly physically, but they can also be fun!

There have been studies done to justify the use of moderate exercise to slow down the damage done by the deterioration of the cardiovascular system. The Paffenberger study of 16,920 men who were all alumni from Harvard indicated that an increase of one to two years of longevity occurred for men more than eighty years old when they exercised moderately throughout their adult lives.[6]

By keeping active, our older church members will not only live longer, but they will also live healthier lives. This will affect their need for surgery, or even their ability to withstand and recover from surgery.

Exercise is not the only thing older adults can do to help themselves. Diet is also important. The effects of a poor diet are seen more as we age than when we were

---

[6]   R. S. Paffenbarger, A. L. Wing, and C. Hsieh, "Physical Activity, All-Cause Mortality, and Longevity of College Alumni," *New England Journal of Medicine* (314): 605.

young. In this case, the sins of our own past will affect us. Fatty foods are a major concern because they can produce heart disease or high cholesterol. The same can be said with our food preparation. When I was a teenager, nearly everyone in the United States fried their food. Many of today's elderly still prepare their food that way. Many Southern dishes are still prepared with the use of animal fat or have fatty meat as a part of the meal. The effects of this fat range from weight gain which can be a factor in diabetes and high blood pressure, to cardiovascular diseases.

Meals prepared by the churches should also keep nutrition and preparation in mind, especially if these meals are a part of a Meals on Wheels program. The effects of high fat or high sodium can be harmful to all of us, especially the elderly.

One of the unrealized effects of a spouse's death is that the remaining spouse usually does not bother preparing well-balanced meals for themselves. If by chance the remaining spouse is a man, he may not have ever cooked! If the remaining spouse is a woman, which is more likely, she often feels like it is a too much to deal with, especially if she has been cooking for "him" all her life.

When people with cardiac problems go to long-term care facilities, they usually require a strict low-sodium, low-cholesterol diet. Sticking to a diet can be one way the facilities are able to reduce the risk of a heart attack. They are also usually encouraged to perform moderate exercise. Most facilities have activity programs that include things like chair exercise. A popular exercise program recently is one called "Body

Recall." Through this program, muscles from the toes to the face are recalled to perform tasks that enable the older adult to live better. Some of these facilities have indoor and outdoor recreational programs. The nursing homes have special physical therapy programs to assist residents in rebuilding muscle tone and function.

During your visits to these facilities, do not bring any food except for the spiritual food they so desperately need. Encourage your parishioners to continue the hard work of exercise and therapy. Be aware of their limitations and do not overstay your welcome.

Cancer

In modern society, cancer is the second leading cause of death. It is compared to the "white death," or tuberculosis, of the eighteenth century and the "black death," or bubonic plague, of the Middle Ages. Cancer has been known and described throughout history, although its greater prevalence today is certainly due to the conquest by medical science of most infectious diseases and to the increased life span of humans.

In the United States in the early 1990s, more than one-fifth of all deaths were caused by cancer. In 1993, the American Cancer Society predicted that about 33 percent of all Americans would eventually develop some form of the disease. Skin cancer is the most prevalent cancer in both men and women, followed by prostate cancer in men and breast cancer in women. Lung cancer, however, causes the most deaths in both men and women.

Cancer is the common term used to designate the most aggressive and usually fatal forms of a larger class of diseases known as neoplasms, which are heritably altered, relatively autonomous growths of tissue. A neoplasm is autonomous in that it does not fully obey the biological mechanisms that govern the growth and metabolism of individual cells and the overall cell interactions. The changes seen in a neoplasm are heritable in that these characteristics are passed on from one cell to its progeny, or daughter cells.

The principle classification of neoplasms as either benign or malignant relates to their behavior. Several relative differences distinguish the two classes. A benign neoplasm is encapsulated, but malignant neoplasms are not. Malignancies grow more rapidly than do benign forms and invade adjacent, normal tissue. Tissue of a benign tumor is structured in a manner similar to that of the tissue from which it is derived; malignant tissue, however, has an abnormal and unstructured appearance.

There are different types of cancer that affect the older adult. I would like to share just a bit of information about each. The first type of cancer I would like to deal with in this section is breast cancer. According to the American Cancer Society, breast cancer is the leading killer of women worldwide. The majority of cases occur in postmenopausal women. When breast cancer is diagnosed, treatment begins with surgical removal of the cancer. Most patients are then given radiation and/or chemotherapy treatments to make sure that all the cancer is destroyed.

No one cause for breast cancer has been identified, but diet is believed to play a role.

Perhaps the best thing we can do as clergy or laity is to be open to listening to the fears and concerns of the women who find that they have breast cancer. Most male clergy cannot relate to this issue very well, but we can be good listeners. It may be good to try to put a newly diagnosed parishioner in touch with someone who has gone through a similar experience. One-on-one support and group support can be very helpful.

The lady with breast cancer is not the only person who may need counseling after a diagnosis. Husbands and adult children may also need someone to hear their fears and concerns. Issues relating to physical disfigurement and loss of intimacy are concerns that must be dealt with by spouses. Children may be sympathetic toward their mothers, but soon they will begin to become concerned about their own health and the possibility that they too may develop breast cancer. Listening ears, one-on-one support, and group support can help all involved through this very trying time after diagnosis of breast cancer.

Lung cancer is caused primarily by smoking. Cigarette smoke contains many initiating and promoting agents, placing at risk smokers and non-smokers who are regularly exposed to secondhand smoke. Genetic factors may play some role in this disease since only about 20 percent of smokers develop lung cancer. By the time this cancer is diagnosed, the cancer has usually metastasized to the point where surgery, radiation, and chemotherapy are not effective.

It is very difficult for some people to be supportive or sympathetic of those who have lung cancer. In most cases, those who have this kind of cancer are responsible for their condition. They are not a "victim." But these church members are addicted and have never been able to get away from this addiction. Support and not reproach is needed here as well.

Prostate cancer is the second most common cancer in men. Unlike many other cancers, the incidence of prostate cancer increases dramatically with age; over 80 percent of all such cancers are diagnosed in men over the age of sixty-five. Like breast cancer, early detection of prostate cancer is important. Unfortunately, the annual rectal examination is still one of the best ways to detect prostate cancer in older men. Treatment of this disease involves surgery, radiation, and the use of hormones and chemotherapeutic drugs. The good news is that prostate cancer patients have excellent survival rates, exceeding 75 percent.

It would be good if you could ask a man who has been one of those 75 percent to talk with someone who has been recently diagnosed. Those who have recovered are living proof that cancer of this type can be successfully treated. A young male or female clergy may have the right answers concerning grace and salvation, but someone who has lived through surgery, radiation, and chemotherapy can offer hope by example. As church leaders, we are aware of who has had what surgery. Keep track. When a situation comes up where you think another church member may be helpful, use his or her to help the elderly minister to each other. For men this is usually a sensitive issue. Be sure you ask someone to visit who is sensitive to the situation.

Skin cancer, one of the most common and preventable cancers, is usually caused by exposure to sunlight. The risk of developing skin cancer can be greatly decreased by limiting skin exposure to sunlight by wearing hats and light-colored clothing or by using sun blocks to prevent the dangerous ultraviolet rays from damaging the skin. The most common types of skin cancer are readily diagnosed, treated, and cured at the early stages. Fortunately, our senior population was not as prone to the notion that the tanner we are in the summer, the better we look. They also lived in a time when the ozone layer over our earth was not damaged, resulting in more ultraviolet rays effecting our exposed skin. On the other hand, more of our seniors worked out of doors than we do today.

Cancer-causing agents, chemical, biological, or physical, are termed carcinogenic. Chemicals that cause cancer have a variety of molecular structures and include complex hydrocarbons, aromatic amines, and certain metals, drugs, hormones, and naturally occurring chemicals in molds and plants. Several drugs used to treat cancer are also carcinogenic; although these chemicals are used to break DNA strands of cancer cells, thereby killing the cells, this same property causes the agent to induce cancer in normal cells.

The most clearly established biological agents, however, are the oncogenic viruses that commonly induce the formation of neoplasms in other animals.

Some of these viruses are linked to human cancers. Oncogenic viruses are divided into DNA and RNA viruses, depending on genome structure. The DNA viruses mainly insert their genetic information directly into the cells of their hosts. The RNA viruses require first that their genetic information be transcribed into DNA by the enzyme reverse transcriptase, supplied by the virus. All forms of oncogenic viruses contain one or more genes that are essential for the transformation of the infected cell into a neoplastic cell. The viral form of the oncogene appears to be activated and expressed abnormally by one mechanism or another, leading to neoplastic transformation of the cell.

Ultraviolet and high-energy radiations are causative agents for human and animal cancer. A correlation exists between exposure to the sun's ultraviolet rays and the occurrence of skin cancer. Cancers caused by radiation include leukemia and cancer of the thyroid, breast, stomach, uterus, and bone.

In general, cancer is not the direct result of genetic inheritance. However, several cancers, including cancer of the colon, breast, and prostate exhibit a familial predisposition, although the inheritance pattern is polygenic or multi factorial. While these types of cancer exhibit a dominant mode of inheritance, they are recessive, requiring the alteration of both copies of the affected gene in order for a cell to become malignant.[7]

The best we can do as pastors is to become knowledgeable about these various kinds of cancers and share that knowledge with our church members.

---

[7]   *Grolier Multimedia Encyclopedia*, s.v. "Cancer."

The majority of cancer is related to the environment. Once we become aware of them, we can work to eliminate them. Knowledge about the disease will give some comfort to the person diagnosed. The pastor can offer knowledgeable support and help set reasonable expectations.

Because cancer is the most feared disease in our society, numerous psychological reactions and problems affect the cancer patient. The delay in seeking medical help for a health problem that the patient fears might be cancer is a tragic example because in many instances delay may mean the difference between affecting a cure or not. This fear is sometimes so great that it results in a tendency toward suicide. Such extreme reactions are unwarranted because the cure rate continues to rise.

Church members with cancer have a variety of psychological reactions related to their own personal background, the kind of cancer they have as well as the site of the cancer. Obviously, the problems become compounded with recurrent tumors because of the greater fear of the outcome and the doubt that a recurrence is not a one-time event. Soon the patient begins to doubt the physician and may even refuse treatment and lose hope. Cancer is a frightening disease, but not a desperate one. Many kinds of cancer can be cured. Education, reassurance from those who have won the battle themselves, love by family and church members, and understanding all help in recovery of cancer. The church has been so helpful to parishioners and families through the years who have suffered from one form or another of this disease. Support groups sponsored by the church are very helpful.

A very active church member in my second appointment made me keenly aware that my support was important, but the support of other church members who have had a similar disease and survived was even more important. Clergy cannot be all things to all people. Many times our parishioners benefit from the love and advice offered by fellow churchmen. Be aware of what your parishioners have endured in the past and help them understand how they can help one another.

My mother's entire family has died of one form of cancer or another. We buried her older brother six months before learning that my mother had cancer. It is a disease that destroys the body. Questions about prayer, the will of God, and obedient living fly about as we ask ourselves "Why?" But cancer happens, even to folks as wonderful as my mom.

In long-term care facilities we do find people with cancer. Many come there because they can no longer live on their own. The nurses treat their needs with appropriate medication and compassion. As they near the end of their lives, oftentimes hospice volunteers are called in to assist the resident. The clergy is usually a part of this team. By being aware of what is happening to the church member, the minister will be able to respond more appropriately.

There is a lady in my current facility that has come there to die. Though she continues to receive treatments, there is little hope. Our job is to assist her through this very difficult time. Her family is not in the area and can only visit on weekends. Special foods are prepared for her due to her lack of appetite and upset stomach from the medication. Encouragement to get up and going comes from the staff. The other residents extend compassion and well wishes. Her minister as well as the chaplain and I offer spiritual support. The atmosphere around this resident is one of great care. I'm sure you would find the situation to be similar in other facilities.

Sight

As we age, we experience more difficulty with our sight. In the long-term care facilities with which I have been affiliated, nearly 30 percent of the residents experience some kind of visual impairment, some of whom are totally blind. More than double that number, about 65 percent, wear eyeglasses to correct their vision. For those residents, these facilities offered large-print books from the library and ensured that menus were also printed in large print. The local church can do the same. Bulletins, newsletters, conference reports, hymnals, devotionals, or any other material you expect the whole congregation to read should either be large enough for the elderly to read or you should provide large-print options for those who do need them. Perhaps audiotapes of services or meetings would work better with those who have sight problems. Many of the elderly are afraid of falling due to poor eyesight, so home visits to them are greatly appreciated. Perhaps the churches should consider official meetings during the daytime or just after worship and lunch as a way to enable the elderly to participate. Many churches have a ride-sharing program wherein someone driving by the home of an elderly church member could stop and pick them up for worship or other events.

Lighting is also an issue of concern for the elderly. Nice, shiny floors may be appealing to us, but to the elderly the glare can present a problem. An older person takes longer to recover from glare than does a younger one. Adaptation to lighting levels, especially early-dark adaptation, takes longer for seniors because the lens of the eye thickens with age, causing less light to pass through and adaptation to be less flexible. A loss in accommodation, called presbyopia, decreases the ability for the eye to focus on close-up objects with age. The pupil diameter becomes smaller, causing less light to enter the eye. Cataracts cause a clouding of the lens and a decrease in the amount of light able to enter the eye. All of these normal changes to the eye as we age present a challenge to the elderly every day. Our houses of worship should consider in their design or remodeling the particular needs of the elderly. More light at entranceways help the older person with the adjustment from a bright sunny day to the inside of a hallway. A low-gloss floor wax helps prevent glare on tile floors. Additional lighting in sanctuaries may enable an older person to read from the bulletin or hymnal.

This concern was brought to my attention in the last assisted-living facility I opened. There were windows in the dining rooms, and we had mini blinds on them along with curtains. When residents started to move in, I noticed that the mini blinds would be closed in the morning. I asked the staff why they were closing the blinds only to find out that it was not the staff but the residents who were doing it. The beautiful, early morning sunshine that I thought would brighten everyone's day was in reality causing some residents to have difficulty seeing!

Let me suggest that you smear Vaseline petroleum jelly on a pair of glasses to simulate the effects of cataracts or dimming eyesight and try to walk throughout your facility. Be careful of the steps and curbs! This experience should also enlighten you to the effects of shadows in hallways and darkened entranceways. Pay close attention to the amount of light that is provided in your facility. Oftentimes, it is not enough to enable those who have sight deficiencies to feel comfortable. There are many elderly who do not wear glasses because they cannot afford them. The Lion's Club is a social organization that raises money to help people who cannot afford an eye exam or glasses. Perhaps your congregation could serve as a drop-off point for used glasses that are recycled into new glasses for someone who could not afford $150 for new glasses. There is a special concern for those older adults who have some dementia. They often misplace things, and eyeglasses are no exception. Their poor eyesight only serves to add to their confusion and disorientation.

Another visual impairment to consider is the yellowing of the lens. As we age, the lens of the eye not only thickens, but also begins to yellow. The elderly person has difficulty discriminating among shorter wavelength colors and has better success with longer wavelengths. Reds and yellows are colors they can more easily discern. If we expect someone to pick a white piece of communion bread off of a white doily, it may be difficult. If we use a color contrast, the older eyes will not have as much difficulty.

To help you better understand the distinctions I have just mentioned, place some yellow foil over your glasses and walk around. It will be easy to see how the yellow changes how all the other colors look.

Contrasts are very important to the elderly eye, especially while trying to navigate hallways that may not be light enough. If the floor is a light color, stairs should be a different color or have an edge that is a different color so the older person can easily distinguish that something different is about to happen here. Many churches like to use red carpeting. The church my family and I have attended for many years has red-carpeted stairs that come from a red-carpeted balcony and lead to a red-carpeted vestibule. This can be quite dangerous for the elderly. Dark colors often are difficult for those who have depth perception problems. Baseboards of a darker contrasting color to the floor will help the older person to know exactly where the floor ends and the wall begins. Handrails or chair rails are also a tremendous help to persons with sight problems. Challenges with depth perception and diminished visual acuity cause difficulty in identifying stair height. Loss in stereopsis (depth perception) can cause problems in locomotion and way finding in the older individual. When visiting in a long-term care facility, offer your arm to the resident and walk a little slower. They may not tell you, but it is more difficult to walk quickly when suffering from the kinds of sight problems I've mentioned here.

My father suffers from a common eye problem that afflicts the elderly. He has macular degeneration. In his case, he has lost the sight in one eye and the middle of the other. As a result, he must look very closely at any object. He tells a story about himself of how, after a move to a new community, he was walking through the neighborhood when a lady was walking by and said hello. He was pleased that the people in his neighborhood were so friendly and so was encouraged to speak first to the next person he saw. He did so, but there was no reply. As he continued to walk, he thought that perhaps he had made too hasty a decision on how friendly the new neighbors were. On his way back to his house, he passed the same person who had snubbed him earlier and he decided to make another attempt to be cordial. As he got closer to the person standing on the side of the road, he realized, to his dismay, that it was not a person, but a fancy mailbox that had been so rude to him earlier!

It is hard to lose one's eyesight. In my current facility, there are five people who had eyesight so poor that the residents have been declared legally blind. They have adapted over the years, but must depend on others to assist them with things like their finances. One resident was convinced that her brother was taking advantage of her by spending her money. She could not see to write checks and could not see the bank statements or returned checks. It is a difficult situation to be in as we age.

When you visit long-term care facilities, be aware of the problems associated with poor eyesight. If you send parishioners bulletins or newsletters, be sure that the font size is appropriate for those who have difficulty seeing. If you expect them to follow liturgy, make sure you have large-print hymnals to assist them.

Hearing

Poor sight is only one of the senses that decline as we age. Hearing is another of our senses that declines. The most common characteristic of an elderly person is that of someone who cannot hear. Some of us have been accused of having selective hearing loss, but that is not the problem many of the elderly face. Presbycusis is a term used to describe any hearing impairment in old age, especially as it relates to high-frequency tones. That is why some older people say, "I can hear him just fine," when referring to a male with a deep voice. For some, louder sounds are hard to distinguish, and consonants become harder to understand.

Nearly 26 percent of nursing home residents suffer from some hearing impairment and about 5 percent are deaf.[8] Many of the poor elderly are unable to afford hearing aids. Those who can afford them often, for reasons that center primarily on vanity, never buy them. Once again, the Lion's Club is a wonderful source of assistance for people who need hearing aids.

Many churches already provide special hearing-enhancing equipment in their sanctuaries, or provide designated seating near the front for those who are "a little" hard of hearing. I had a retired minister in the

---

[8]   James Allen, *Nursing Home Administration* (New York [Springer Publishing Company], 1992), 466.

first church I served who not only sat up front, but had a hearing aid as well. As I began to preach each week, he would reach up and adjust his hearing aid. I never knew if he was tuning me in or out. Another exercise for pastors that would help them better understand what it is like to be elderly would be to place cotton in their ears and try to stay attentive to conversations or worship services. You will find in a hurry that it is easier to grin and nod your head than it is to keep up. May I suggest that all meetings use some kind of amplification so that everyone is able to hear? If you are visiting an older person, pay special attention to them to try to discern if they understand what you have said. Perhaps you could ask questions that would require a response rather than a nod to see if you need to talk a little louder. Many times people who wear hearing aids in public take them off at home. If you do not normally make appointments but simply drop by to visit an elderly church member, you may want to be sure you are being heard from the beginning of the conversation.

My first appointment beyond the local church into long-term care ministry was to a facility that was under construction. Having lived in a parsonage in another state, we had no home waiting for us, so my family and I used four rooms in a newly opened facility owned by the company I was with while our house was being built. To this day, my daughter remarks about how she was awakened each morning at 6:00 a.m. by the sounds of the lady in the room across the hall who was hard of hearing. The staff would shout at her to communicate, and she would turn on her television at full volume as she began to get ready for her day.

Many older people have been misdiagnosed as having dementia because of their slow or inappropriate response to questions, when in reality they were hard of hearing and misunderstood the questions. It is very important that the elderly get and wear hearing aids to enhance their own quality of life as well as that of those around them.

One resident of a facility I managed used to sit in the front lobby because she liked to see the activity, but she was hard of hearing. She would oftentimes talk out loud to herself, usually repeating the phrase, "I don't know." One day this repetition got on the nerves of another resident, who hollered out at her to shut up. Suddenly, everyone else in the lobby began applauding! It must have been bothering them just as much.

On my way out of the facility where I work now, I noticed a humming sound. I stopped to investigate. It sounded like it was coming from the heating vent. As I began to snoop around, a resident who was sitting nearby asked what I was doing. I told her about the noise and asked if she noticed it. She said no, and then added that she did not have her hearing aids in. At that moment, I knew where the sound was coming from. The hearing aids were in her purse, squealing!

Sleep

As people age, normal age-related changes occur in sleep patterns. They often find it difficult either to fall asleep or to sleep without waking several times each night. The result is that they are tired.

Sleep apnea is defined as cessation of breathing for over ten seconds at least five times in an hour. This often results in an awakening and can seriously disturb sleep. As many as 25 percent of all seniors may fit this categorization, most of whom are are men. The most successful treatment for sleep apnea is wearing a mask that applies positive pressure to the airway and keeps it open.

The church where I worship some time ago had an older gentleman who had been notorious for napping during worship. Occasionally the clergy would tease him about it, but the napping did not cease. Being aware that some of our elderly members may suffer from this problem may enable you to discuss the possibility of treatment or physician consultation. I would also encourage you to make your pastoral visits to the elderly short. Short visits more often serve those who happen to nod off better than a long visit.

Pressure Sores

Often when the older adult loses the ability to ambulate, they spend more time in a chair or even bed bound. Some may be bed bound as a result of a stroke of other incapacitating disease. With prolonged bed rest, oftentimes the elderly develop bedsores, pressure sores, and stasis ulcers. Tissue breakdown often occurs over a bony prominence like a hip, elbow, or heel. Many times the older adult will develop these sores while hospitalized for treatment of other conditions. The prolonged constant, unrelieved pressure creates the tissue breakdown. The tissue breaks down from the inside to the outside until the outer layer of skin opens. These areas are not only uncomfortable for the elderly person, but also serve as a possible sight for infection.

I have seen many residents in the nursing homes and adult-care facilities I have served who have bedsores because they were not rotated in bed from one side to another to relieve the pressure in a given area. I have seen skin break down as a result of poor hygiene. Those people who are incontinent of bowel or bladder suffer from skin breakdown just as children would if they were not changed regularly.

People who have these conditions require a special treatment from nurses to help the healing. It takes time. During that time, since these are open wounds, infections can set in and cause more problems. My advice to clergy and laity who visit an elderly person with pressure ulcers is to make your visits short so as not to interrupt the turning schedule that is designed to give relief and assist in healing. If there is some kind of an infection in a wound, be careful. If there is a sign on the door telling you to wear a gown, gloves, or a mask, do it. You are not immune to becoming ill just because you represent the Lord! And though we all think we are fine, germs we carry to someone who is already ill may cause further illness.

Arthritis

For many elderly, arthritis is a condition they live with every day. Arthritis is an inflammation of a joint. There are several different kinds of arthritis but all have the effect of causing pain in the joint where it is found. It is most common in the fingers and knees, thus impeding locomotion and the use of the hands. From my experience, I would estimate that at least 25 percent of nursing home residents suffer from some form of this disease. Of course, one does not have to be in a nursing home to have it, nor do they have to be elderly, but this, like all the other conditions mentioned thus far, is found predominately among those who are over age sixty-five.

When visiting with the elderly, be aware that they may have difficulties with their hands or other joints. Simple things like buttoning a dress or tying a shoe can be a problem. I had one lady tell me that picking up one of those small pieces of communion wafer was too difficult for her. I began to use real bread when visiting the shut-ins after that.

Falls

In a recent study by Kennie and Warshaw, it was determined that more than 70 percent of the deaths that result from falls occur with people age sixty-five and older.[9] It is very easy to understand how this could happen. Older people living alone may fall down the

---

[9]   Ibid., 494.

steps, slip in the tub, or, as I identified in an earlier example, fall and break a hip.

I remember seeing a resident in my first assisted-living facility walk across the lobby, stop, and turn to look down the hall, and, in that simple movement, break her hip and fall to the floor. The physician explained that in most cases of a broken hip, the break actually occurs before the fall because the bones of the elderly are so brittle.

Falls are the most common incident reported in long-term care facilities. Most of those occur in the room of the resident. More often that not, the falls occur in the bathroom or near the bed. I constantly get reports about the nurse finding a resident sitting on the floor due to a fall. Fortunately, most of these falls result in no injury, but sometimes they do cause a broken hip or elbow. The problem occurs when surgery is necessary for a ninety-year-old frail person. I have had some people who have gone to the hospital for just such a surgery and never come back.

A common problem among the elderly is orthostatic hypotension. This is simply being light-headed when you rise from a bed or chair too quickly. Oftentimes this leads to dizziness that results in a fall. For the elderly who suffer from orthostatic hypotension, the best advice is to stand up slowly and stay standing for a few seconds before beginning to walk.

A first-alert kind of a program, where the elderly person wears a necklace with a device to call for help when they have fallen, is a wonderful idea. People seldom fall near a phone, and a broken leg or hip will be very painful if one tries to move. It would be a good ministry for the church to form a calling chain where church members call each other every day to make sure they are all right. The elderly can be a part of this chain too, enabling them to be a part of this ministry. For those who are unable to come to worship any longer, this is a good way of helping them stay in touch with the active congregation. News, joys, concerns, and prayer needs can be relayed via the phone. Checking up on one another can be a valuable ministry for those who may find themselves in need as well as for those who are making the calls.

Anxiety

Anxiety is something everyone experiences. We all learn to cope with it in our own way. The elderly too have reasons to be anxious. They are concerned about issues of safety, health, family, and future. I will address the issues of anxiety over the future in a later chapter, but the other concerns need some attention here.

Safety is a concern among the elderly because they oftentimes live on their own and consider themselves more vulnerable. In addition, they realize that "I'm not as young as I used to be." They are often in ill health and are many times non-ambulatory. They know they are frail and easy prey for a younger, stronger person. As a result, the elderly oftentimes do not like to go out after dark. They prefer to go with someone else.

The second thing that produces anxiety among the elderly is concern over health. Throughout this chapter, I have been identifying some of the medical conditions that are common among the elderly. Heart, lungs, diseases, and frailty are all reasons for concern. Chronic illnesses and dehydration are constant reminders that the elderly are getting older. They get concerned about their medication, which one to take when, and what it does. Most older adults have something "wrong" with them because bodies age and parts wear out. Therein lies the reason for anxiety.

This is just as true for folks in a long-term care facility as it is for anyone else. Sometimes I think that the residents in my facility talk more about aliments and doctor's appointments than any other single topic. It seems as if the one with the most problems wins somehow. They seem to delight in topping each other with what is wrong with them at the moment. Of the two concerns that I mentioned above, safety is the highest-ranked reason the residents give for coming to the facility where I work. The second highest is assistance with medical needs. They do worry about these things, and many times do so for good reason. Oftentimes, people suffer from high blood pressure and need someone to be sure they take their medication. Some of my residents are diabetics and need special attention in giving the correct dosage of insulin along with a proper diet. Indeed, safety and health are major concerns for the elderly. Being sensitive to these concerns will improve one's ability to serve as a pastor.

Sexual needs

Sexual needs persist into old age, with continued activity considered healthy and health preserving.[10] The elderly continue to have needs for a positive self-image and self-esteem, which are closely associated with the needs for intimacy and sexuality.[11]

Sexuality is not achieved exclusively by sexual intercourse but may also incorporate a variety of activities related to touch and displays of affection.

In the facility where I served as the director, I had a couple that celebrated their seventy-fifth wedding anniversary. The building was designed to have the couple sleep in separate bedrooms within a suite. The two decided that they would rather sleep together. They asked me if I could remodel the suite in some way as to enable them to have one large bedroom rather than two smaller ones. The man said to me, "Just because we are in our nineties does not mean we do not have sexual relations." It is indeed true that some couples have sexual relations all their lives. Some modifications may be required, but it is possible.

I recently attended a seminar on aging where the physician indicated that the frequency of intercourse among twenty-year-olds was nightly; among thirty-year-olds, every other night; among forty-year-olds, weekly; among fifty-year-olds, two times a month; among sixty-year-olds, monthly; and among seventy-year-olds, weakly. A survey conducted by the American

---

[10]   Ibid., 503.

[11]   Ibid., 503.

Association of Retired Persons found that more than six in ten men between the ages of forty-five and fifty-nine and a similar percentage of women the same age reported having sex at least once a month. One in four people over age seventy-five reported similar frequency.[12]

As pastors we need to know that there are changes that occur to our bodies as we age that make sexual intercourse more difficult. Men may require more time to attain an erection, and ejaculation may decrease in force. Orgasm may not even be experienced during intercourse. Women experience thinning of the vaginal walls and reduced vaginal wetness and elasticity. It may take longer for older women to respond to sexual stimulation, and orgasms may be less pronounced. In spite of these normal complications, there are many things the older couple can do to be sexually fulfilled.[13]

I have identified several of the physical conditions that the elderly church member may experience as they age. Those of the congregation who are shut-ins or who live in a long-term care facility have greater physical needs than those who live independently and continue to shop, drive, and come to worship. Not all elderly experience all the things I've talked about but they are

---

[12]   *Virginian-Pilot*, August 5, 1999, A5

[13]   Nancy R. Hooyman and Wendy Lustbader, *Taking Care of Your Aging Family Members* (New York: The Free Press, 1986), 140.

the most common, with the exception of what I will discuss in the next chapter, on the nervous system and the many problems that the elderly may face in this regard as they age. Hopefully, this information will be useful as we minister to the elderly and design ways the elderly can remain an active part of the ministry the church provides.

Chapter Three
The Aging Nervous System

Anyone who keeps the ability to see beauty never grows old.

In this chapter, I would like to look at the nervous system and especially the brain in relation to the aging process. Though the other parts of our bodies are important for clergy to understand, the brain and its potential aging difficulties will give us greater clarity in interpreting the behavior of many of our elderly church members.

There are normal changes that occur in the nervous system as we age. One major misconception about the aging brain is that neurons are lost daily and that at advanced ages there are half as many as when we were young. A statistic frequently heard is that we lose 100,000 neurons a day. But what we do not hear is that the brain normally contains a trillion neurons. So even if we did lose 100,000 a day for each of the 365,000 days in a 100-year life span, that would still be only 0.5 percent of the total with which we started. That seems hardly significant. Successful brain aging results in some loss of complex reaction time and speed in responding to questions, but no major losses in the ability to learn, remember, or perform routine mental tasks.

Psychologists have identified two kinds of intellect. The first, fluid intellect, represents limits imposed by the mechanics of the central nervous system. It is independent of the content to be learned. It is inherently biological and there are genetic differences in performance based upon this type of intellect. This kind of memory does decline with age. Crystallized intellect represents the facts, rules, and procedures we have learned over our lifetimes and our strategies for solving problems. Crystallized intellect involves reading, writing, and judgment. Only very late in life does the crystallized intellect decline. If we continue to challenge ourselves intellectually, it should increase over most of our lives

One of the major brain-related problems that seem to plague the older adult is the high risk of a cerebrovascular accident (CVA), more commonly known as a stroke. The stroke is the most debilitating accident an elderly person can face. In the United States, 400,000 people have strokes annually, with one-third dying as a result. Strokes are the third leading cause of death. Many older adults suffer from strokes that have caused memory loss or paralysis. The cause of strokes is lack of oxygen to the brain. Blood carries the oxygen, so the lack of oxygen is usually the result of blockage of a major blood vessel called thrombotic strokes, or perhaps the leakage of blood from a vessel that has ruptured, called hemorrhagic strokes. It is estimated that 60 percent of the cerebral vascular accidents are due to arterial thrombosis.[14] Hypertension is a major culprit in hemorrhagic strokes. If blood clots occlude a vessel very briefly, they may cause a transient ischemic

---

[14]   Ibid., 466.

attack (TIA). TIAs are usually defined as temporary neurological deficits, which resolve within several hours. I will talk more about the effect of these "mini-strokes" later.

In many patients, there is partial recovery of the functions normally served by the damaged area, presumably because of transfer of these functions to other regions of the brain, which remain intact. Theoretically, this requires some reorganization of the synaptic connections within the brain. The damage to the brain affects our bodies in many ways.

Treatment of stroke involves several stages. The first involves minimizing the initial stroke damage. Recently, a clot-dissolving drug was approved for treatment of thrombotic stroke. This drug works best when administered shortly after the stroke. The second stage of stroke treatment is the recovery stage. Here, physical, speech, and occupational therapy are extremely valuable. Encouraging the stroke patient to stick with the hard work demanded of them by the therapists is very important. There seems to be a critical time frame after a stroke when plasticity is occurring. If new functions are not regained during this time frame of a few months, the stroke victim may never recover. The third stage, often concurrent with the second, is to control the risk factors for further strokes. Reducing hypertension, correcting high cholesterol, cessation of smoking, and beginning a physical exercise routine can all reduce the risk of future strokes and heart attacks. Reduction of alcohol intake and control of diabetes are also valuable. Studies have shown that aspirin can decrease the potential for platelets to form clots. In some individuals, a surgical procedure, carotid endarterectomy, may open narrow regions of the major artery to the brain and reduce stroke risk.

As church leaders, it is important that a stance is taken regarding our bodies and what we do to them. Having the information in the above paragraph, it is clear that we need to take a stand on alcohol abuse. It may be a good first step to let our church facilities be used as a meeting place for AA. With all the news regarding smoking and the law suits against major tobacco companies, it should be clear that tobacco is not good for us and that it is also addictive and therefore hard to simply "give up." It might be a good idea to begin a support group for those church members who want to stop smoking but need some help. A physician may speak to a group about how best to go about "kicking the habit." Offering help, support, and encouragement to our members who struggle for their health is certainly a positive sign to all who see that your church cares about people.

Some of the common results of a stroke may be aphasia, which is the inability to interpret and understand words, or dysphasia, which deals more with the inability to speak and paralysis of one side of the body, leaving the person unable to walk or use one arm.

If stroke victims are uncomfortable coming to worship, sending a cassette or videotape to their home will help them continue to feel like they are a part of the congregation. It would be even better if specially trained laity could take the materials along with a bulletin at an appointed time to share "worship" with the stroke victim.

One of the residents of an assisted-living facility I managed suffered a stroke. Her right side was paralyzed and her speech was affected. She was a delightful lady who had been a faithful church member. Though she could not speak, she was a faithful attendee at our weekly chapel services. One day, we were singing a hymn, and this lady began to sing! We were all astonished. In this case, she could not form the words she was thinking, but could sing the old hymn that was part of her long-term memory.

There are people who have suffered from a stroke in nearly every congregation. Having handicap access enables these church members to continue to participate in worship. We must be attentive to their special needs. Someone who uses a walker may not have enough room between the pews in the sanctuary. They could sit down front, of course, but that seat is reserved for the pastor's family! The simple act of standing for hymns may be difficult for someone who uses a walker. They need the walker for support. Without it, standing may not be very easy. The pews we have in most of our congregations do not offer any arms like a chair would to enable the older person to push himself up. Perhaps it would be good to reserve the end of the pews for those who need this added assistance. Another option would be to buy stackable chairs with arms that can be placed strategically through the sanctuary for our older members, especially those who have suffered a stroke. When we share the Eucharist, most denominations ask the congregation to come to the front of the sanctuary around a communion rail. Someone with a walker would find this difficult and may feel like they were holding others up. In like manner, when we offer an altar call, the person who has suffered a stroke may find it too difficult to make his way to the front. I encourage you to borrow a walker and try to make your way through the crowd to say good morning to the pastor one Sunday. Use it during worship and you will soon be going to the worship committee to talk with them about changes needed in the order of worship as well as sanctuary design.

Physical conditions like those that result from a stroke are easy targets for people who like to make fun of an others' inability to walk or talk. It behooves the church to learn how to deal with our brothers and sisters who have suffered a stroke, and to serve as an example of how to love those who make us feel a bit uncomfortable in their impairment.

If stroke victims are made to feel uncomfortable coming to worship due to physical conditions or attitude, they will not come back. They may choose to stay at home because it is simply easier to do so than to deal with the many obstacles we place before them. In that case, sending a cassette or videotape of the service to them will help them still feel like a part of the congregation in some small way.

Dementia is a term that broadly defines cognitive loss. Nearly half of all dementia is a result of Alzheimer's disease. Twenty percent of all dementia is due to multi-infarcts, "mini-strokes." Another 15 percent is a combination of Alzheimer's disease and strokes. The remaining 15 percent is made up of other diseases like Parkinson's, Huntington's, Creutzfeldt-Jakob, Pick's, and depression.

Alzheimer's disease, the largest cause of dementia, is a progressive brain disorder affecting memory, thought, behavior, personality, and eventually muscle control. It is estimated by the Alzheimer's Disease and Related Disorders Association, Inc., that the disease affects as many as four million Americans.

Symptoms of Alzheimer's disease include a gradual memory loss, decline in ability to perform routine tasks, disorientation in time and space, impairment of judgment, personality change, difficulty in learning, and loss of language and communication skills. The disease eventually leaves its victims unable to care for themselves.

As mentioned earlier, the Alzheimer's Association estimates that four million Americans have the disease. Ten percent of those adults over age sixty-five have the disease. Forty-eight percent of those adults over age eighty-five have the disease. The Association states in its statistics sheet published in 1993 that Alzheimer's disease is the fourth leading cause of death among adults, that it primarily affects people over age sixty-five but can strike people in their forties and fifties, that someone with the disease can live from three to twenty years, and that the cost of home care for someone with the disease averages about $18,000 per year.

This is indeed a costly disease, monetarily and emotionally. Many families try to meet the needs of their elderly parents. The typical pattern is to hire someone to act as a caregiver in the home of the parent, where he or she is most comfortable. Oftentimes, problems arise as the disease progresses and the need for oversight becomes a twenty-four-hour-a-day job. The next step usually is moving the Alzheimer's victim into their home with them so that they can watch them in the hours they are not working. There are many adult day care centers available these days that will accommodate the Alzheimer's victim. These programs offer a degree of assurance because they eliminate the fear of a caregiver not coming to the house due to illness. As the disease progress, incontinence often becomes a problem. Difficulties arise with wandering away from home. This disease often also affects ambulation. For many people, an institution such as an assisted-living facility or a nursing home is the final answer. Each step along the way is more costly emotionally and financially than the one before.

The first person I ever met with Alzheimer's disease was a well-known minister I remembered from my youth. At the time, I was working as a student intern and visiting the shut-ins in a church-related nursing home. I saw his name on the door and looked in to say hello. His response was a string of words that would embarrass a sailor. I was dumbfounded. I must have been standing there with my mouth hanging open because a nurse took me aside and explained to me that he had Alzheimer's disease and that sometimes judgment is impaired, resulting in profanity that would otherwise have been kept in check.

I was the director of my first assisted-living facility with a "special needs" unit for adults with dementia. One day, a woman and her son came to visit. I showed them the facility and explained all of the available programs and options. The lady was so weak that I found her a wheelchair to use during the tour. I was under the impression that she as looking for a facility for herself, but when we visited the "special needs" unit she explained that she was looking for a facility for her husband. The dear lady had worn herself out trying to care for him at home. Her physician finally insisted that she find a facility for her husband, who was in good physical health, so that she could regain her own health.

Unfortunately, there is no known cure for Alzheimer's disease. There are currently two drugs that have been approved to treat Alzheimer's: Cognex and Aricept. Both of these medications work by increasing the availability of a brain chemical called acetylcholine, which is involved in memory. These are treatments and not cures. They can produce improvements for a short while and are used most often when the victim is in the early stages of the disease. The hope is that through research, a cure will be found soon so that the four million people who currently suffer from this disease will be the last.

The Alzheimer's Association issued a report of ten warning signs that depict in many ways the inability of the disease victim. The first is that those people who have dementia not only forget things, but also do so more often and do not remember them later. A second sign is difficulty performing familiar tasks. People with Alzheimer's disease could prepare a meal and not only forget to serve a dish, but forget that they cooked it all together. Problems with language are identified as a third sign of the disease. The Alzheimer's victim may forget simple words or perhaps substitute inappropriate words, making conversations very difficult to follow. The fourth sign noted is disorientation of time and place. Someone with Alzheimer's disease may get lost in his own neighborhood and not have any idea how to get home. Though it is not restricted to demented people, poor or diminished judgment is the fifth warning sign. The victim may forget they are dressed and add another layer or a second or third hat. They may not wear anything at all. Many of us have problems balancing our checkbook, but oftentimes the Alzheimer's victim may look at all those numbers and forget what they represent. Abstract thinking is developed as we age and is very difficult for a demented person. Perhaps the thing that we think of first when we see Alzheimer's disease is forgetfulness in that we misplace items. Oftentimes, misplaced items are found in some very unusual places. Rapid mood swings or behavior changes are also a sign of the disease. The ninth sign is similar to the previous one, but deals with personality changes. Often Alzheimer's victims become distrustful or paranoid. It is often true that folks like retired clergy end up swearing and acting ugly, which was not their nature before developing the disease. The final warning sign for Alzheimer's victims is a loss of initiative. They lack the desire to begin new projects or to do anything on their own. I have found that it is good to know these signs because they help me better understand the world in which the Alzheimer's victim lives.

Try to use these warning signs as a basis for planning ministry to church members who have dementia, especially of the Alzheimer's type. Visit often, but do not expect them to remember you. They will remember what they learned as a child and young adult. Their faith will not be developed as one might expect, but they have the faith development of a teenager or earlier. Music, prayers, and songs learned as a child will be retained. Symbols like the cross or candles or stained glass still carry a lot of meaning for them. Communion may mean a lot even though they may not be able to participate verbally. Try to educate your congregation to be accepting of these victims so that they may be able to continue to worship with the congregation.

What can the church do for victims and families in the midst of this struggle? Oftentimes, families become embarrassed by the behavior of the Alzheimer's victim. They stop coming to worship. It is very difficult to get someone else to come to their home and watch the victim while the spouse goes to worship because their behavior is often unpredictable and many people are afraid of what they cannot manage.

In the early stages of the disease, Alzheimer's victims are often tearful because they realize that there is something wrong. As the disease progresses, anxiety and agitation become more prevalent. Depression is one of the next things that become obvious, along with purposeless activities like pacing or tapping. Suspiciousness and paranoia go along with delusions that often occur as the disease progresses. Many times there is a fear of being left alone and verbal outbursts that may make no sense. These kinds of behavior are common in people with Alzheimer's disease. The question is: "How can we minister to people who behave like this?"

There is, with this disease, the temptation for people to ask, "Why me?" as if God had punished them by afflicting their loved one with Alzheimer's disease. The disease is so debilitating and so far reaching in its effect of family and friends that it is easy to see it as a punishment. There are families who have felt much like Job and wondered what they had done to deserve this.

Multi-infarct dementia is similar to Alzheimer's disease in that it produces a loss of intellectual function, but the reason for that loss is different. In this case, the loss is due to multiple strokes (infarcts) in the brain. These strokes may damage areas of the brain responsible for a specific function and can also produce generalized symptoms of dementia. Someone who suffers from multi-infarct dementia may be paralyzed on one side *and* display loss of memory or exhibit poor judgment. Like Alzheimer's disease, multi-infarct dementia is not reversible or curable. The use of brain scanning techniques, such as CT scans and MRIs, can identify strokes in the brain and further identify this particular kind of dementia. Those who suffer from multi-infarct dementia have some days that are better than others regarding recall and judgment, but as the brain suffers more and more damage from these mini-strokes it will decline in much the same way an Alzheimer's patient declines. Slowly but surely, the brain is destroyed by small blood clots. The effected area dies from lack of oxygen and glucose.

Parkinson's disease is a progressive disorder of the central nervous system that affects more than one million Americans. Those who have Parkinson's disease lack the substance dopamine, which helps control muscle activity. Late in the course of the disease, some Parkinson's victims develop dementia and eventually Alzheimer's disease. Conversely, some victims of Alzheimer's disease develop symptoms of Parkinson's disease.

Huntington's disease is an inherited, degenerative brain disease that affects the mind and the body. The disease usually does not begin until mid-life and is characterized by intellectual decline, involuntary movements of arms, legs, and facial muscles, personality changes, memory disturbance, slurred speech, impaired judgment, and psychiatric problems. Huntington's disease affects more than 25,000 Americans. Although there is no treatment to stop the progression of this disease, the movement disorders and the psychiatric symptoms can be controlled by medication.

Creutzfeldt-Jakob disease is a rare, fatal brain disorder that is caused by a transmittable infectious organism. The symptoms of Creutzfeldt-Jakob disease include failing memory changes in behavior and a lack of coordination. As the disease progresses, mental deterioration becomes pronounced, involuntary movements appear, and the victim may become blind, develop weakness in the arms or legs, and in time lapse into a coma.

Pick's disease is another rare brain disorder that like Alzheimer's is difficult to diagnose. Disturbance in personality, behavior, and orientation may precede and initially be more severe than memory defects.

Depression in the elderly is more common than many people believe. It is estimated that the lifetime risk for depressive disorder is on the order of 10 to 15 percent. It is invoked by sadness, inactivity, loss of appetite, difficulty in thinking and concentration, feelings of hopelessness, and sometimes suicidal tendencies. Depressed persons often have some mental deficits that include poor concentration and attention. Those who suffer from depression oftentimes experience loss of memory of "how to" perform certain functions, the ability to recognize people they have known for years, and the ability to speak.

Some degree of depression after a major loss is relatively normal. When you think about this age range, sixty-five plus, you know there must be major losses encountered during these years. Death is a constant companion. Spouses, parents, friends, and even children may die during these senior years. There is also the loss of jobs, identity, house, and positions in the community. These are major losses with which most seniors will deal. However, if these losses cause depression that is so severe as to interfere with the activities of daily living or extend beyond six months, the person may be a candidate for treatment.

A man and his wife made arrangements to move into the assisted-living facility where I work. Before they could move in, the man had a heart attack and went to the hospital. Upon discharge, he moved into the suite prior to his wife. She would stay at home for a few weeks and continue to prepare to make the move. A few days later, he had another heart attack and died. His wife eventually moved in as planned but she became very depressed. Her only daughter had died six months earlier. Her husband had died. She had moved from a home she had lived in for thirty-five years. She had been a golfer and enjoyed her days at "the club," but she did not drive and could not go there by herself. She also had been a smoker, but was not allowed to do so in the facility. Her life was completely changed. It is no wonder that she became depressed. She had three major changes within six months and she was lost. She felt alone. She talked about suicide but was afraid that if she killed herself, she would not be reunited with her loved ones in heaven.

Day after day she talked about her plight. Many times a day, she cried and told anyone who would listen about how much she missed her daughter and husband. It got to the point that other residents would ignore her because they had heard her story so many times. They too had issues and concerns. But with the help of some medication, visits from her pastor, and time, she was able to become less anxious, more independent, and far less depressed. As time went by, she would tell me that she was feeling a little down, but was improved from what she felt for several months after coming into our facility.

Dr. John Taylor, at a recent seminar I attended on depression, indicated that for those who are over age eighty-five, men are twelve times more at risk of depression than women are. Protestants are more likely to commit suicide than others. Those who are deeply religious are less likely to commit suicide than others. Whites have a higher suicide rate than non-whites. Married people are less likely to commit suicide than those who are single. Those who are blue-collar employees or who have low-paying jobs are at greater risk than the converse.

One of the potential problems depressed adults face is alcoholism. Those who are depressed often turn to alcohol as a means of self-medication. The stresses of aging, with its losses and depression, can lead to suicide or alcoholism. White males living alone and who are depressed are most likely to turn to alcohol. Those elderly who are both depressed and alcoholics are five times more likely to commit suicide.

This helpful checklist will assist in determining if a parishioner is depressed. The key is to ask if any of the following symptoms have persisted for than two weeks. If four or more of these symptoms are present, you should refer this parishioner to a doctor.

___A persistent sad, anxious, or "empty" mood

___Loss of interest or pleasure in ordinary activities including sex

___Decreased energy, fatigue

___Unusual irritability

___Excessive crying

___Recurring aches or pains that do not respond to treatment

___Sleep problems such as oversleeping

___Eating problems such as loss of appetite or weight loss or gain

___Difficulty concentrating, remembering things, or decision-making

___Feelings of hopelessness or pessimism

___Feelings or guilt or worthlessness

___Thoughts of death or suicide

The depression that occurs without a precipitating event is called endogenous depression. In its most severe form, it is virtually incapacitating. The victim loses desire to get out of bed, to eat, to put on makeup, or shave. There is no motivation to do anything. In these cases, the intervention of a physician is necessary.

Clinical depression is a whole body disorder. It can affect the way you think as well as the way you feel, both physically and mentally. For those people who are sixty-five or older, as many as three out of one hundred suffer from clinical depression. It can be serious and in many cases even result in suicide. The good news, however, is that nearly 80 percent of the people with clinical depression can be treated successfully. Even the most serious depressions can be managed with the right combinations of medication and therapy.

There are two types of clinical depression. The first is major depression. In this case, it is impossible to carry on usual activities such as sleeping, eating, or enjoying life. One is consumed by the depression and becomes more and more lethargic. This kind of depression may occur once in a lifetime or may occur several times over. Only professional treatment can help a person with this kind of depression. A second kind of clinical depression is bipolar disorder. This depression leads to mood swings from extreme lows to excessive highs. These swings occur in cycles and are controlled with medication. The high part of the cycle is called mania. The low part is depression. While manic, the person seems to have boundless energy and enthusiasm. The opposite is true while depressed. This kind of depression usually starts when people are in their twenties. It requires continual treatment to keep it in check.

I had a parishioner who suffered from manic depression. She would take her medication for a while and feel fine. Then she would stop taking it because she thought she was better. The cycles of highs and lows would start all over again.

There are multiple treatments available that accelerate recovery from depression. Cognitive and behavioral psychotherapy have benefit in treating mild depression. A variety of anti-depressant medications are now available. Each has its value and some have negative side effects. As pastors, our job is not to play doctor but to encourage our church members to visit their physician for assistance during this difficult time.

Depression has classically been viewed as increasing with age, but some recent data indicates just the opposite. Though age does not seem to be a determining factor, sex does. Women are reported to have depression more often than men overall.

How can the church minister to people who have one or more of the diseases I have mentioned above? Symbols of the church may still carry meaning to people with dementia. Music can be soothing for the demented adult. Religious songs that have been sung since childhood may be recalled in spite of some kinds of memory loss. Fellowship is important to everyone, but large crowds are difficult for the demented to handle. They may become agitated because they are not sure what to do or how to act. They are confused. Small groups and one-on-one visits are much better ways to have fellowship with the demented. Sunday school class members or choir members could provide pastoral visits to the demented adult who no longer functions well in a hall or worship setting. These adults require our help. We need to minister to them and their needs. Their spouses and families need our assistance, physically and emotionally. Picking up a few groceries for a friend whose spouse is demented is easy for us, but greatly appreciated by the families. If we could give the spouse a break during the day for him or her to run some errands, they will come back refreshed and better able to deal with the frustrations that come from caring for a demented adult twenty-four hours a day.

When I was the executive director of the Hampton Roads chapter of the Alzheimer's Association, I received a phone call from a man who said, "Talk to me before I hit my Dad in the face." This caregiver was at the end of his rope. He was so frustrated because his father was irrational, never seemed to pay attention to what he was just told, and insisted that he needed to go home for dinner.

Our support should be for both the victim and the family. Home health nurses or parish nurses can be a very practical kind of program for a church to begin. Nurses who understand dementia can be trusted to care for our elder church members. Adult day care programs are another service churches can offer to the elderly and their families. Many churches already have childcare centers or preschool programs. Adult day care centers are similar. In fact, complement each other in many ways.

The last local church I served had both a childcare center and an adult day care center. Some of the adults volunteered in the childcare center as "baby rockers." They would spend time each day in the infant room, sitting in the rocking chairs, humming or singing softly to the child they held. There was supervision, of course, and only those whom we thought were able to perform this task were selected. For those who were selected, the effect of rocking and singing was quite calming. Though they were confused, nearly every one of our "rockers" was able to perform the task, and both they and the babies benefited.

In that church, we started a support group for the children and spouses of those adults who came to our day care center. Not all our adult day care clients were demented, but most were there because they needed some sort of supervision. Once a month we met and featured someone who could provide advice, information, or comfort to families that were struggling with feelings and concerns about their loved ones and their current situations.

It is nearly impossible to fully appreciate the plight of a demented adult. The greater the degree of brain damage in given regions, the more memory is destroyed. The following exercise may help stimulate your thinking about the needs of the demented adult.

Imagine that you wake up in the morning. You look around and you do not know where you are. Next to you in bed is someone whom you do not know. You need to use the toilet but do not know where it is. So you begin to roam around the house filled with strange things and many doors. There are too many doors, too many options. You do not find the bathroom because you are not sure if you were going out of the room or going into it, and you check the same door several times. You do not find the bathroom in time. You wet your underwear, pajamas, and footies. This is uncomfortable and embarrassing and so you take them off and begin to search around for someone or something that is familiar. Though you do not know where you are, you know where you should be: at home, the home you lived in years ago. Eventually you find the kitchen and look for some food. There is a toaster, so you look for some bread. When you put the bread in the toaster, you forget about it (out of sight, out of mind) and continue to look for something else, something that may seem familiar. Finding nothing, you go out the door onto the sidewalk. Not knowing which way to go, you decide on a way and begin to walk. At the end of the block, you cross the road and nothing seems familiar. Cars go by, models you do not recognize. People go by and look and stare at you. You cannot remember where you were, but do remember where you want to go. And so you continue walking, not sure you are going the right way, but you continue to walk.

If you were in a facility like an adult-care facility or a nursing home, the scenario would be a little different. Someone in a uniform might come into your bedroom to wake you for a bath before breakfast. You may not know them and wonder why they are in your bedroom. Where is your spouse? Someone says, "Good morning," but you don't recognize him or her. They tell you it is time to get up and change your diaper and get a bath. You are not sure you want some strange person touching or washing you. You protest. The person talking to you seems nice enough and does seem somewhat familiar. She insists that you get undressed. You do not want to get undressed, changed, and bathed. You refuse. You tear off your diaper and get out of bed. Though unsure where you are, you are sure that you want no part of the person in uniform giving you orders. You start to go to what must be an exit, to get away, but the lady with the clean diaper in her hand stops you and tells you to come with her toward another door. You do not know what is behind that door, but you know that you do not want to go there. You pull your hand free, hit the lady, and run as fast as you can out the door from which you were just pulled away.

The days of these two demented adults you were imagining being oftentimes get worse than the ten minutes I took you through in the exercise. They may include police picking you up or medication that makes you sleepy. All of it is frightening and strange. None of it makes any sense to you. And you ask constantly for someone to give you an explanation only to forget it and ask for it once again.

Long-term care facilities deal with demented residents in a variety of ways, but it seems that special units or wings are now common in an attempt to meet the unique needs of the demented person. They require constant attention and assistance. I was asked to help design a unit for a company I worked for, and we spent a great deal of time going over all the needs of the residents. Then we began to talk about space requirements, colors, furniture, closets, keys, and a wide array of things that must be considered as we try to meet the unique needs of the demented adults. Often the demented resident becomes incontinent, so placement of the bathroom within eyesight of the resident is important. Some demented residents will dress and undress several times a day, so closets that lock are important. Restless residents need safe places to walk with places along the way to stop and sit or interact. Dining is often a challenge; therefore, a larger space than normal is necessary, as are extra caregivers to help feed those who need this help. Time and date reminders are always important, as is a special activity program that meets the needs of the active and passive resident.

Chapter Four
Healing

*Years wrinkle the skin, but to give up hope wrinkles
the soul.*

I have been sharing a lot of information about aging
and diseases that affect the elderly, but I would remiss
to not also share some information about healing and
recovery from illnesses. We who are Christians believe
that our God can and does lend healing. It gives us hope
in the face of despair and confidence to move on after
trauma. I have known for years and have witnessed
for myself in my own family, in my ministry in the
local church, and in my ministry to the elderly that
faith can help in the healing process. We have all seen
the miracles of healing when all hope was gone, but
what I would like to talk about is the not so miraculous,
but significant healing that occurs every day with our
elderly church members.

There was an article in the October 1998 issue of
Readers Digest by Malcolm McConnell that talked
about how faith can heal. In that article, McConnell
relays a study done by Dr. Harold Koenig, an associate
professor of psychiatry at Duke University. As a
result of studies done on thousands of American
since 1984, it was determined that "religious faith
not only promotes overall good health, but also aids
in recovery from serious illness." According to Dr.
Koenig, through prayer, religious patients "acquire an

indirect form of control over their illness." The article indicates that those who attended worship at least once a week spent, on average, about four days in a hospital, while others who did not attend as often spent ten to twelve days hospitalized. This information has been confirmed by other studies around the world that see health benefits related to post-surgery recovery, heart attacks, and strokes. McConnell noted a study done at Yale University that looked at over 2,800 people over the age of sixty-five. Those who never or seldom attended worship "had nearly twice the stroke rate" as those who attended regularly.

The physiology involved in the healing that has been noted begins with a reduction of stress. My family practice physician has told me that 75 percent of the patients who come to see him have a stress-related illness. Heart disease, hypertension, panic attacks, asthma, insomnia, and many more illnesses and diseases have stress as a major factor in their occurrence. We know that prayer and especially meditation can relieve stress. One of the things I learned as a tool to meditation was the value of repetitive prayer. It helps us center in and focus, but at the same time it slows us down. Our heart rate decreases, our breathing slows, we relax and remain relaxed as we pray.

Dr. Koenig discovered in his studies that stress impairs the immune system. When we are stressed, our body creates an inflammatory agent called interleukin-6, which, according to Koenig's study, is "associated with chronic infections, diabetes, cancer and cardiovascular disease." Koenig found high levels of interleukin-6 in the blood levels of those who seldom or never attended worship. On the other hand, those who attended worship on a regular basis had significantly lower levels of interleukin-6 in their blood. The obvious conclusion is that those who pray cope better with the stress that confronts us all.[15]

Most of the diseases that are affected by stress are diseases most associated with the elderly. Heart disease, cancer, and diabetes are common among the elderly. Perhaps the church could make an effort to impress upon those who are middle-aged the importance of prayer and faith in creating good health. For the elderly who are afflicted by these diseases, the power and practice of prayer can be very beneficial.

Faith, healing, and good health go hand in hand. The last assisted-living facility I directed was very much aware of the need for healing of body, mind, and spirit. We made devotions, worship, and prayer a part of our everyday lives. I was never surprised when our care plans revealed that a resident was doing better and needed less medical attention. We tried to minister to our residents in a holistic manner. I believe that central to Jesus' teachings is a concept of love that is fundamental in all our interactions with one another. It is the basis for giving care, for receiving care, for healing, and for future hope. Jesus understood love as complete devotion to God and to one another. Experiencing God's love enables us to love others in return. This can easily be translated into caring for the elderly, the ill, and the infirm. We assist the healing

---

[15]   Malcolm McConnell, "Faith Can Help You Heal," *Reader's Digest* (October 1998): 109.

process through our love and devotion. We encourage good health through good nutrition and exercise. We enable faith to grow through devotions, worship, and one-on-one conversation. The church can do the same for its members in a wide variety of ways.

The role of the local church pastor in this healing process is essential. Visits to facilities where a parishioner is living are very important. Encouragement to get well, to do better, and to hang in there is essential in the healing process. You would be surprised to learn how important a visit from a minister is to the older adult who is in a long-term care facility. They look forward with pride and anticipation to the day when their minister is to come. They share their news with those who dine with them, tidy up a little more, and do their best to be prepared for the visit.

An older minister friend of mind told me that one of the things he did as a nursing home chaplain was to make appointments with the residents before he left. He was convinced that it gave the resident something to look forward to in what can be lonely days.

Nutrition

The elderly are believed by some to require fewer calories in their diet than when they were younger because of a reduction in body weight, a decrease in metabolic rate, and a decline in activity. These factors do suggest a need for fewer calories, but at the same time there is an increased demand for nutrients to help the elderly resist the effects of disease. Unfortunately, many elderly do not bother fixing a good meal for themselves, especially if they are single. They end up eating what is easy or quick and are not as concerned as they should be about the nutritional value of the food. There are many vitamin supplements available that can help the elderly person remain healthy.

One way our society has found to help the elderly stay healthy is through a Meals On Wheels program. Healthy, warm meals are brought at noon to the homes of the recipients. Most programs offer an additional sandwich for a lighter evening meal. All of the Meals On Wheels programs I have known have been church related. A church or a group of churches prepares the meals and serves them. The meals act not only as a means of providing good, warm food, but also as a point of contact from the church to the parishioner. In many cases, this contact is the only one the elderly person may have all day.

Some churches use these meal deliveries as a means of checking to ensure that the elderly are okay. I am aware of at least two occasions in the programs I have related to, the alert delivery volunteer prompted police and medical attention for elderly women who had fallen and broken their hips. Because they lived alone and could not move, they were unable to get the assistance they needed.

Nutrition and healing go hand in hand. There are many diseases that can be treated with certain kinds of foods. Vitamin E is necessary for good eye health. The mineral iron in dark green, leafy vegetables is important for many people as they age. Iron is an essential part of all cells. Low-sodium diets are common for the elderly as a means of keeping blood pressure in check. Low-fat and low-cholesterol diets assist those with cardiovascular problems. High-fiber diets often are necessary for good digestion and regular bowel movements. Diabetics have a difficult time healing from bed sores or surgery. Paying special attention to their diets helps them in their everyday life as well as in healing.

Chapter Five
Types of Elder Care

In spite of the cost of living, it's still popular.

Oftentimes our older church members get to a point in their physical or mental condition where they need some assistance. There are five basic types of care offered to the elderly. The church can be of assistance in all of these levels of care. But it seems obvious that when people are still in their own home, the church can be of greater assistance than when they are a part of an institution that has the responsibility to care for the church member.

The first kind of care available to the older adult is the kind of care they can receive in his or her own home. I have mentioned earlier the Meals On Wheels type of programs regarding nutrition. Some churches have these kinds of programs, where meals are prepared in the church kitchen and distributed throughout the community to those in need. This is very helpful because the older person often does not cook for himself or herself like they did when there was a family to prepare for and eat with, or even when there was a spouse involved. Their nutritional intake is oftentimes not what it should be. These meals enable the older adult to say home a little longer.

In addition to the meals that are so very helpful, some churches have a visiting nurse program or a parish nurse program wherein a nurse who is a member of the congregation visits to assist the older member with bathing, dressing, or taking their medication. For those who are a little forgetful, this visiting nurse can be especially helpful. With their supervision, medication will be taken as prescribed, alleviating the need for hospitalization due to the inappropriate use of medication. One need not be a nurse to bathe someone or help him or her get dressed. It takes only a few minutes each day to assist a neighbor in this manner.

If the church cannot offer assistance in this manner, there are many professional organizations that will provide nurse aids, licensed practical nurses, and registered nurses to perform designated tasks. By having these people come into the home, the elderly person retains his or her independence and remains in a comfortable setting. My advice is to be sure to check out the home care provider before they are hired. Criminal background checks and checks on current licenses are very important.

The church can also be helpful in identifying people who have a difficult time living alone. Perhaps two church members would like to try living together to conserve resources and share responsibilities. Oftentimes having a companion in the house can stimulate activity, lead to better nutrition, and enhance socialization.

A second kind of care has become quite popular over the past few years. It is called, for lack of a more dignified name, "adult day care." In this case, the older adult may continue to live with one of his or her children and go to adult day care during the day while the children go to work, or just to give them a day or two to relax or do the many things that are required of us all. The advantages here are that quite often these day care programs are church related, many housed in an educational building or social hall of the church.

Oftentimes it is possible for an older person to remain at home if there is an adult day care center for the family to use. These are places where an older adult can spend several hours or an entire day. Adult day care is particularly helpful to the families of persons with a form of dementia. They provide supervision, socialization, activities, and meals to those in attendance each day. Many also have a health care component that assesses and monitors the participant's health care needs. There is usually a daily fee for the services found in adult day care centers.

The stimulation and interaction the older person receives can noticeably enhance his or her functioning level and quality of life, while providing the family member or caregiver with assurance that a loved one is safe and secure for those hours of the day.

In the church I served in Pittsburgh, we had a childcare center and, as the need became apparent, developed an adult day care center. One of the unique opportunities that evolved from having both these programs was that we often had older adults volunteer to rock the little children. It was a tremendous intergenerational program. The babies and the adults both enjoyed it.

The third type of care available for the elderly is assisted living. In this case, the older adult moves into a facility that is designed to meet their needs. The facility will provide housing, meals, and assistance with all the activities of living such as, medication, ambulation, bathing, dressing, eating, and grooming. They also provide housekeeping and laundry service, and most often have an extensive activity program that includes worship and devotions. In these assisted-living facilities, there are nurses who provide the care twenty-four hours a day. Most often, if the resident needs assistance, there is a way to call for help so that the resident feels comfortable.

These kinds of facilities may also be called "personal care homes" or "adult homes." They require a written agreement between the resident and the facility, a history and physical exam by a physician, and an assessment that results in a personal care plan for each resident. The staff members in these facilities are trained to provide the necessary care.

Some state board most often gives a license to assisted-living facilities or personal care homes. They have strict regulations for all areas from construction to care. Many of these facilities accept Medicaid reimbursement for the care of their residents. The rate is different from that paid to nursing homes because the services offered are different.

Some people will function well in this environment for many years, but others may need the kind of services only offered by a nursing home. This is our fourth level of care for the elderly. Jeff Gelles, who writes for Knight Ridder Newspapers, had an article in a local newspaper in July of 1998 about long-term care insurance. He said, "A 65-year-old woman has a 1 in 2 chance of spending time in a nursing home; for a 65-year-old man, the chance is 1 in 3."[16] That statistic is pretty significant. Now that does not mean they will stay there forever. Some will go to a nursing home for rehabilitation after a fall or a stroke. Others may go there to regain their strength after a lengthy hospital stay. These kinds of facilities offer intensive nursing care for the elderly. Other reasons for going to a nursing home may include the need for a G-tube or NG tube for feeding, the need of a ventilator for assistance in breathing, IV therapy, the control of a communicable disease, or treatment of severe bed sores. These facilities offer care that one cannot get at home or in an assisted-living facility. As a result, they must be concerned about infection control, proper nursing procedures, proper diets, and safe environments. With these as priorities, the facilities cannot look like one's home. They must look a little more institutional. Nonetheless, each nursing home does make an effort to make the resident comfortable by providing activities, gift shops, and furniture that is less like what you may find in a hospital.

Most nursing facility residents are unable to care for themselves on their own. In addition, many have chronic illnesses or were transferred from a hospital following a serious illness, accident, or operation. Each facility will have its own application form that requires disclosure of personal, financial, and medical information. A doctor's order certifying the need

---

[16]   Jeff Gelles, "Long-Term Care Insurance Is Best Bet For Some But It's Costly," *Virginian-Pilot,* July 27, 1998, D4.

for nursing care is required for admission as well as a comprehensive assessment for those applying for Medicaid assistance at time of admission. Like the assisted-living facility, nursing homes also have admission agreements, and care plans are prepared to tell the staff what kind of assistance the new resident needs.

A popular alternative to the separate facilities I mentioned above is a "continuing care retirement community." Continuing care, sometimes called life care communities, typically offer a variety of independent living arrangements for residents together with medical and nursing services, full, central dining accommodations, and educational, recreational, and social activities. Residents may be offered maintenance services for their major home needs, which help to create a comfortable retirement community atmosphere. This type of care is the fifth and final.

Residents in these communities are most often required to pay a sizable entrance fee as well as a monthly charge in return for all the services offered and use of their living accommodations. Some agreements between the residents and the community may state that medical and nursing care will be made available to the residents without any increase in the monthly charges. Some communities charge additional specified fees for these more costly services.

The biggest advantage to this type of community is that one can move in while relatively healthy, live in a nice, safe community in a villa or apartment, get home health nurses to assist them, if necessary, move into the assisted-living unit if necessary, and eventually move into the nursing wing when and if health needs change. They would continue to be among friends and not have to worry about where they would go if medical assistance were necessary. They seem to be growing in popularity, and I anticipate that they will continue to do so.

These five levels of elder care are designed to meet particular needs at particular times in the lives of the older person. It would be helpful for the minister to know a little more about these five levels of care and what is available in his or her community. Many denominations provide assisted living, nursing homes, and continuing care retirement communities as a ministry to their members. It is popular these days to offer a campus setting for the elderly, whereby when one needs additional assistance he or she simply moves to that level of care within the campus. If yours does not, or if it is located so far away that your members would not use it, I would recommend that you make an effort to visit those that are nearby. Take time to talk to the director or administrator about the kind of service they provide. You will be better informed when a parishioner comes to you seeking advice in the future.

While we are on the subject of long-term care, it is important that I share just a little information with you regarding costs for this care. All five levels of care can be paid for in private funds. Oftentimes, Medicare will pay for in-home nursing assistance if it is around certain areas of care that can only be done by a registered nurse and is called for by the doctor. Medicare will also pay for the first ninety days of therapy in a nursing home. But Medicare does not currently pay for any part of adult day care or assisted-living fees, unless it is home health care that is required to come into the facility just as it would be required in one's own home.

In a draft issue of a report on long-term care regarding financing printed in October of 1998 by the Joint Commission of Health, the following information was shared. The average cost of a nursing home stay in the state of Virginia in 1998 was $79.56 a day. The primary payment source for this kind of care was Medicaid. Medicaid is the federal program that pays for residents who have a very small income. The average cost for assisted-living facilities in the state of Virginia in 1998 was $31.92 per day. Medicaid was once again a primary source of payment. Twenty-two percent of all assisted-living residents living in Virginia were residents who received a Medicaid payment for their stay. Adult day care costs in Virginia averaged $34.50 per day in 1998. Once again, Medicaid was the primary source of income.

Long-term care insurance is an increasingly common means of payment to assisted-living and nursing facilities. This insurance pays a set amount per day for care in these facilities. The patient would have to pay the difference. Some policies also cover home-based care where a home health nurse comes into the home to provide services.

None of these insurance programs are open-ended. They all have a limit on the number of days and the amount they will pay per day. Many people will not be able to afford to stay in either of these facilities without the sale of their homes or other property. Even at that, they may run out of money and have to seek Medicaid assistance to pay for their stay.

I have identified many types of care offered to the elderly and talked a little about costs. It is important that the clergy understand all these options. When you go to visit the shut-ins of your congregation, learn as much as possible about their conditions and concerns. You may be able to act as a resource for families who are unfamiliar with all the options I have introduced you to above.

Ministry to and with the Elderly

Chapter Six
"Over My Dead Body"

Accept the changes age brings and stay alive inside.

I have just shared with you some of the types of care available to the older adults. In this chapter I would like to spend some time looking at the issues involved in leaving one's home and moving into the home of a relative, a retirement community, an assisted-living community, or a nursing home.

"Over my dead body" is usually the first response when the subject of leaving one's home to move into an institution is brought up. The response is understandable to some degree. We like to be independent. We enjoy our freedom. It is an embarrassment to have to admit that we are no longer able to take care of our home, our financial affairs, or ourselves.

The move from one's own home to a retirement community may be the least difficult of all of the moves we can make as an older adult. Though it is "institutional" in some ways, the person moving in still retains their own space, their "home." It may be an apartment or a cottage but it is theirs and they still make many of the major decisions. Services are provided such as housekeeping and a meal plan, but one is still rather independent. Often people living in these communities are still able to drive, go on vacations, visit whomever they please, go shopping, and do all the things they used to do in their own homes. The move to this kind of an institution is in some ways like moving into a condominium with some extra services available. As time goes on and the needs of the older person increase, this kind of community is able to offer additional services. This knowledge is helpful in making a decision to leave one's home. There is only one move required for the rest of your life.

Moving in with children means leaving their own home where they are in control and living in a room in a house owned by someone else. Mother-in-law suites have become a popular add-on to homes in an attempt to provide closeness as well as independence. Older people often resist this move because they don't want to be a burden to their children. My parents took in my grandmother after my grandfather's death. Though they provided a suite complete with kitchen, bath, living room, bedroom, and porch, it still was not quite the same. My parents felt like they had to be at home or take my grandmother with them if they went somewhere. And Grandma felt like she was holding them back from enjoying their retirement years. The obvious advantage of this kind of an arrangement is the ability of the child to provide care or assistance to the adult. Housekeeping, laundry, and meals can be provided if necessary. Medication administration is also often a need for those who have some mild dementia. In spite of the problems that can and do arise, for older adults this is an alternative that meets with less resistance than moving to an assisted-living community or nursing home.

It usually takes some sort of a major event to encourage people to leave their home and go someplace else to live. Many times it is a hospital stay due to inappropriate usage of medication, or malnutrition, or perhaps a fall while getting into or out of the bathtub that prompts older adults to seek out a facility that can meet their needs. The decision to leave one's home is seldom easy. Oftentimes the children of the prospective resident of an assisted-living community are those who have to make the decision based on what they believe is best for their parents, or perhaps out of exhaustion from trying to care for them for many years as the older adult's needs increase. The church and especially the clergy can be helpful in the struggle to make this kind of a decision. The children and the parents both need support and encouragement. Children often feel guilty for not taking their parents into their own homes or for "giving up" and parents do not want to be a burden. If the church could pay a little attention by listening to the emotions that are expressed by both parent and child, they would provide a valuable ministry.

In the last assisted-living facility where I was the director, we were aware of the many reasons why someone would not want to leave home, so the building was designed to meet these objections. The large facility is broken into smaller neighborhoods for ten to twelve people. Some of the rooms were two-bedroom suites, while others were smaller but still large enough for a couple to share a living room, bedroom, bath, and kitchenette. The smallest suite was a one-bedroom designed like a studio apartment including kitchenette, private bath, and bedroom. Small living rooms, kitchens, TV lounges, and dining rooms were located in each neighborhood. We had a chef who prepared the meals to ensure that they were tasty and met special diets, an activity director who provided about twenty-four hours a week of activities, a car to take people to appointments and shopping, and nurses for each neighborhood to ensure resident safety and to provided needed services. The laundry was done for one person at a time in small, stackable washers and dryers to ensure that clothes did not get mixed up. There was a beauty shop, a physician's exam room, a prayer room, courtyards, and screened-in porches available for the residents to use. Our goal was to enable the residents to live as independently as possible for as long as possible. We tried to appeal to those who were relatively healthy by providing a beautiful community combined with the ability to meet some of the special needs the older adults may have.

In spite of the wide array of services and amenities this beautiful facility provided, I still heard comments like "I'm not ready for this yet" or "These people are too old for me." Most often those who offered the objections were just as old as our current residents were. The need was not there yet.

The move to any kind of a facility encompasses more than just concerns for independence. It also includes concerns regarding loss of home, of furniture, of memories of things familiar. Though people are often encouraged to bring their bedroom suite and possibly some living room or den furniture with them when they move into an assisted-living facility, there are still many possessions that are quite meaningful to them that they cannot bring. China, dining room suites, and pianos are just a few. In addition, the flowers planted years ago, the bird feeders where the cardinals feed, the large oak tree with the swing hanging down are things that hold fond memories. The step that creaks, the window painted shut, and the attic full of "important" things are all difficult to leave behind.

One man told me recently that he did not want to come see my facility because he didn't want anyone telling him when to get up or when to eat or when to bathe. He wanted to make those decisions himself. His comments reflect the fear that many people have about institutional living. They assume that there is no room for flexibility and that everyone has to do everything at a certain time in a certain way. It is true that there are meal times, but most assisted-living facilities offer a range of time to be seated and do not require that you eat if you do not want to. Many also offer kitchenettes for those who are not morning people and would prefer to fix their own breakfast when they do get up and going.

Concerns about independence, loss of home and possessions, and an unwillingness to conform to communal living are three often-voiced reasons for not wanting to enter an assisted-living community.

These same concerns are also voiced regarding nursing home admissions. But in addition, people have such a negative impression of nursing homes. These facilities serve the very ill, many of whom are incontinent of bowel and bladder. There are odors associated with these conditions that are offensive to visitors. When they visit a nursing home, they are confronted not only with the odors but also with the sights of people in bed and wheelchairs. They see people who are handicapped and deformed. They see people on ventilators and oxygen. They see people with bags full of urine hanging from their wheelchairs because they have been catheterized to enable them to pass their urine. These are not pretty sights. The odors are not pleasant. They combine to create a negative impression, and most people don't want to be reminded that they too are vulnerable, that they too might some day be in a similar situation.

As a nursing home administrator, I heard many people tell me that nursing homes were okay, but that they would never go to one. In fact, I do not recall ever hearing anyone say as they were wheeled in the front door, "Oh boy, I've waited all my life to come to a place like this!" They are not the vacation spot of choice, but they do meet a need that cannot be met at home or in an assisted-living facility. The role of the clergy here is to be supportive of the families who are feeling badly about leaving their loved one in a place they have been told they never wanted to go to. It is to be encouraging of the resident who finds himself in a place they never wanted to be in. It is to visit those who are away from home and loved ones and who are not happy about their current physical condition or their situation. It is to bring God's presence into a situation where people ask themselves every day if there is a God.

"Over my dead body!" Nobody likes change. Nobody likes loss. Nobody likes to be dependent.

Nobody likes to conform. Nobody likes offensive odors and frightening sights. Nobody wants to move into long-term care facilities. But they do because they have to. Those of us in the business try very hard to make their stay a pleasant one. Pastoral care is needed to assist these residents as they struggle with remembering that they said, "Over my dead body," and yet here they are, stuck in a semi-private room with a stranger who snores.

Ministry to and with the Elderly

Chapter Seven
Dealing with Loss

*The tide of life is sometimes very rough, but each
storm we survive makes us better sailors.*

I was talking with a couple several years ago who
were about to retire. They were excited about the
prospects of travel and leisure time that lie ahead. When
I visited them recently, I got a different reaction. The
lady of the couple called her retirement days "a time
of sorrow and pain." My reaction was disbelief. How
could someone who has freedom to do what they want
when they want be in pain? How could someone who
now has the time to visit his or her grandchildren and
travel be sorrowful? But when I listened to this couple
for a while, it was easier to understand how there could
be sorrow and pain.

The "happy retirement" also brought with it many
losses. There was a loss of income, and so a change in
lifestyle. There was a loss of identity. The husband in
this couple was typical of most men in that he identified
himself with his work. After retirement, there is a loss
of identity and, in some cases, a loss of worth or value.
These are only two of the losses this couple went
through, but when you consider the age of the person,
it becomes plain that those over age sixty-five suffer
many losses in the years that remain of their lives. It is

most often the case that one's parents die, if they have not already, when their children are in this retirement age. In the normal progression, spouses who have not already will also die during this time frame. And, though it is less common, many times parents in their older years suffer the loss of their children through disease or accident. Though retirement may be a time to move to a warmer climate, such a move brings with it the loss of a house, a home, and a space that is full of memories. The loss of health is another loss commonly endured by the elderly. With the physical decline also may come mental decline. These losses, along with all those that have already been mentioned, produce stress, grief, and anxiety.

When a person's health declines to the point that they must enter a long-term care facility, unless it is for short-term therapy most people assume the move is the last one they will make. For many people, this is true. Perhaps that is why it is resisted so much. Unfortunately, most often the elderly enter the facility directly from the hospital because it has been determined by the physician or their family that they can no longer live independently. They suffer many losses upon admission to a facility that affects their feelings and behavior.

The first loss, of course, is the loss of familiar surroundings. Oftentimes the elderly have lived in their current home for twenty years or more. Their homes are filled with furniture they have accumulated and used for forty years. Favorite pictures and easy chairs have made their house a home. Memories surround every piece of furniture, every cracked dish, every pair of slippers or sweater sent for Father's Day and Mother's Day over the years. To leave "home" is a major life adjustment. It means leaving so much of oneself, against one's will, to go to a new unfamiliar place. It means adapting oneself and one's lifestyle from living in eight rooms to only one room.

A second loss that is encountered when an elderly person enters a long-term care facility is the loss of family contact. The family does not feel as free to drop by to visit anymore. Without the extra bedrooms, it becomes expensive for family who live out of the area to visit. As a result, they come by less often than they did before. When they do come to visit, the room is too small for everyone to sit in and there are usually only one or two extra chairs for guests. As the elderly person becomes frailer and more infirm, they may require medical attention or become confused, and the family members feel less and less comfortable coming to visit.

I have had numerous conversations with families of demented residents who shared that they find it very difficult to visit because the resident no longer identifies them as a spouse or child. They are not the person they used to be. Their personality has changed. Their behavior can be embarrassing. The family gets fewer rewards out of visiting and simply stops coming.

A third loss suffered by those who are institutionalized is the loss of contact with friends. Usually, by the time someone is admitted to the adult home or nursing home, they are past retirement age.

The average age of those in the nursing home where I worked was eighty-five. Most of their friends were the same age. They too were frail and elderly and did not usually get out to visit. When they did, what they saw in the facility reminded them that they too could be in a similar situation.

Friends from Sunday school or the neighborhood should make an effort to visit as often as possible. They need to plan to do so, perhaps once a week or every other week at a particular time. If they are able to schedule the visit, the person in the facility can make sure he or she is available and ready for the visit. I shared earlier about the friend of mine who was a chaplain at a nursing home. He told me that he always set a time when he would be back to visit the person he was with before he left. His contention was that it gave the person to be visited something to look forward to until the time arrived. When he shared his philosophy with me I was reminded of several of the shut-in members of the congregations I served who were prepared for my visit when I came to share communion. They had the coffee table covered with a white cloth, the Bible out from which to read, and refreshments prepared for us to share. By setting an appointment ahead of time, I could be sure that the person was going to be home, not at the doctor or on another necessary trip. Planning ahead then gives the older person something to look forward to and it ensures that the pastor does not waste time.

The fourth loss experienced by every person who enters a long-term care facility is the loss of control over his or her life. Life in a facility is run on a schedule. There are times to get up, eat, take medication, participate in activities, and take a bath. The more incapacitated one becomes, the fewer options are given to them. Doctors and nursing staff dictate what will be done when and in what manner. Food that had been prepared a certain way for forty years is now being prepared by someone else who does it in a different way. Routines that have been developed over the years are now changed to meet the routine of the facility.

I remember explaining to a ninety-six-year-old lady in a facility that we do not fry chicken because fried food was not good for her. She just laughed and said, "I've been eating fried food all of my ninety-six years. I guess it hasn't been too bad for me." She got her chicken fried that night!

Perhaps that hardest part of living in a facility is sharing a room with someone. Going from a house to a room is bad enough, but having to share that room with someone else is even harder. There is no privacy, and room for very few personal things. The "things" that help establish our identity and remind us of our past are gone. It is indeed hard.

In the nursing home where I did my training, we had a new resident who did not like the room to which she had been assigned. It was too cluttered with her roommate's wheelchair and other personal belongings. We moved her to a second room. The room was better, but the roommate played her TV and radio too loudly. Rather than ask the roommate to please turn the volume down, she asked for another room change. When we finally got to the bottom of these and numerous other complaints, it became clear that she simply did not want to be in a nursing home, and if she had to be in one she certainly did not want a roommate. But what the residents in these facilities do not know is that Medicaid does not pay enough money for everyone to have a nice room all to themselves. The nursing home where I trained actually lost money every day on Medicaid reimbursement. It was only by virtue of the private-pay residents that we could offer even a semi-private room for the poor elderly. Nonetheless, the issue for the facility operator, the social worker, and the pastors to remember is how this kind of move makes the new resident feel.

In addition to the other losses mentioned above, some people also suffer from physical losses that precipitate this institutionalization. Hip replacements due to severe arthritis, leg amputation due to circulation problems and sugar diabetes, strokes, and accidents bring the elderly to a long-term care facility. Some are there for a short time, but for many, this kind of placement is most appropriate. If you couple loss of home with loss of limb, it is easy to see that the elderly in this situation need an extra amount of attention and support from their pastor and church.

The church can be very helpful in the transition from home to the long-term care facility. Pastors who are aware of the many concerns of their parishioner can visit, phone, or send cards or audio and videotapes to the parishioner. Church members can be alerted when a member goes from their home to a facility and encouraged to visit as soon as possible.

As I have worked with people over the years, I have come to identify six major types of loss. Those mentioned above can be placed into one or another of these types of loss. The first is material loss: the loss of a physical object or of familiar surroundings to which one has an important attachment. Leaving a house one has lived in for many years to go to an assisted-living facility or a nursing home can create this kind of loss. The second kind of loss is relationship loss: the ending of opportunities to relate oneself to, to talk with, share experiences with, make love to, be in touch with, settle issues with, argue with, and otherwise be in the emotional or physical presence of a particular human being. It is easy to see how those over age sixty-five can face this kind of loss with their parents, spouses, children, and friends. A third kind of loss is intra-psychic loss: losing an important image of oneself, losing the possibility of what might have been, abandonment of plans for a particular future, the dying of a dream. This is entirely an inward experience. How often have we heard people say that when they retire they will do one thing or another only to have plans change due to circumstances not planned on earlier? It may be his or her own physical health that fails, or responsibilities to provide care for a parent. Their dreams are unfulfilled, and so they grieve. The fourth kind of loss is functional loss: loss of one of the muscular or neurological functions of the body. Strokes, heart attacks, cancer, and diabetes all cause this kind of loss. Strokes that cause the loss of the use of speech or limbs are very difficult for people to accept. Role loss is the fifth kind of loss. This is when one experiences the loss of a specific social role of one's accustomed place in a social network. We have talked about retirement as an example of this kind of loss. But oftentimes, when our spouse dies, we no longer feel comfortable in our circle of friends who are still couples. The last kind of loss is systemic loss. This loss is the destruction of the "system," that is, family, work, or government. Death of a spouse or loved one can change a system like no other. We all have known couples where each performs certain tasks. Upon the death of one spouse, the "system" breaks down. The remaining person from the couple has to develop a new system.

Along with the various kinds of loss I have identified, there are other variables loss may include. There is the avoidable and the unavoidable loss, the temporary and the permanent loss, the actual and the imagined loss, the anticipated and the unanticipated loss, and finally, leaving and being left. By thinking through these variations and being aware of them and how a church member may need a particular kind of attention during specific kinds of loss, clergy will be better prepared to serve their congregations in their times of need.

All losses require the help of the church because the church represents not only a social support but also a spiritual support that can be found nowhere else. Pastoral care and support from church friends help the elderly go on in spite of the many difficulties they face. The church needs to be prepared to offer them assistance. Do we have a rite of passage ceremony for those who retire? Is there any spiritual significance to this decision and action? Are there ways to celebrate career service or dedication? Do we have any unique groups to which the retired are welcomed?

In the last church I served, there was a group of men who got together to provide maintenance to the building on a regular bases. They called themselves the "Upper Middle Age Men's Consortium." Membership to the group was only possible upon one's retirement. The men spent as much time on coffee and doughnuts as they did on the work, but it was a wonderful fellowship and support group for men leaving the workplace and searching for a new identity.

What does the church do for its members whose parents, spouses, or children die? Is there a bereavement support group? Does the pastor go to visit? Are there laity trained to provide pastoral care these situations? Does the choir or Sunday school respond to these crises with food or personal support?

Churches which have programs such as the Stephen's Ministry or the Equipping Laity for Ministry Program are able to provide support to those in grief over a number of months or even years. This support is very important in the grieving process and is central to what a Christian fellowship is all about. Selected gifts are recognized in the laity, nourished, and used to serve the Body of Christ.

Clergy are very busy people. There are numerous demands on their time. The Sunday morning worship service and its preparation consume many hours each week. It is interesting, however: I seldom hear a layperson, when talking about a minister, refer to a sermon delivered or a particular worship service that touched them in any meaningful way. They most often say something like what I heard a young mother tell her little girl. "Honey, this is Rev. Paul. He came to see you the day after you were born. He held you before Granddad did!" The child looked up in awe and admiration. Pastoral care and support make a difference to those in need. Clergy need to provide pastoral care, especially during traumatic, stressful, faith-testing events. It is especially at this time that laity turn to the church for support and guidance. It is imperative that the church be there for them.

Thus far, I have been talking about a variety of losses, all of which are important, but in reading recently about stress I came across a survey by Holmes and Rahe that indicated the single most stressful event in our lives is the death of a spouse. You know this is true. If we take this a step farther, we also know that the average age at which people die in our country for both men and women falls within this sixty-five-plus age group we have been talking about. For that reason, I will pay particular attention to the loss caused by death in the following paragraphs.

When we consider death as loss, we must begin with understanding of terms. Grief is the emotional, behavioral reaction of the person who suffers the loss. Bereavement is the reconciliation or perhaps the integration of this loss in our lives. It is a process that follows grieving. The reconciliation takes place a little at a time until finally we are able to say that we are over the grieving and have accepted the hurt that accompanies loss. Mitchell and Anderson in their book *All Our Losses, All Our Griefs* say that grief is universal, inescapable, even when its existence and impact are denied. It is a composite of powerful emotions confronting us when we lose someone or something we value. It is the work we engage in that enables us to eventually live full, satisfying lives.[17]

I believe that there are certain dynamics of grief. Grief emotions tend to be grouped into five different clusters. The first of these emotions is emptiness. This may include loneliness or isolation. When we feel empty, we feel somehow diminished from within. Loneliness is the sense that one's surroundings are also empty of any of the people who matter or care. Isolation is the sense of being defined from others by some invisible boundary. A second dynamic of grief is fear and anxiety. Prior to the anticipated death of a loved one, we may feel the dread of abandonment. Afterward, we experience the anxiety of separation. We ask ourselves, "What am I ever going to do without him or her?" The third dynamic of grief deals with guilt and shame. As you can imagine, guilt is a dominant component of grief. We feel guilty when we assume responsibility for the loss, made decisions that may have in some way hastened the loss, or have not had an opportunity to resolve hurt feelings in our relationship with the person who has died. As church leaders you have heard these kinds of comments often. Anger is the fourth dynamic of grief. When the loss is death, the

---

[17] Kenneth Anderson and Herbert Anderson, *All Our Losses, All Our Griefs* (Philadelphia: Westminster Press, 1983), 36-46.

anger is oftentimes directed at other family members, medical personnel, or God. In a workshop on activating the inactive church member, I heard a theory that said that when pushed hard by anxiety, people react like either skunks or turtles. Those who are skunks spray all over everyone else (blaming them), while the turtle draws back and blames himself. In these cases where someone suffers loss, I have found this illustration to be true. Sadness and despair are also dynamics we see often in grief. It is normal to feel sad over the loss of something. The degree of sadness is usually equal to the kind of loss. But when sadness is coupled with a sense of futility about the future, that is despair. When people find themselves in a state of despair, pastoral intervention is necessary quickly. Our job is to provide hope, to encourage, to give the parishioner a reason to go on. When an older person is left alone due to the death of a spouse, they sometimes give up, thinking they have no reason to go on. A job helping in the office, or calling on the shut-in, or folding the bulletins can give them a sense of being needed. These dynamics of grief can be found in small or large degree depending on the loss and the circumstances of it. When we think about the elderly and death, once again, they will suffer more from loss than any other age group. Helping them deal with these losses should be a priority of the church's pastoral ministry.

Through the years as I have talked to the elderly, I have found that the major dynamic of the inner experience of grief is that of anxiety. All of the behavioral responses that we observe in grief, including fear, seem to be related to anxiety. If anxiety is the perception of a threat to ourselves, then it is easy to see how it relates to fear. Being in a situation similar to one that caused harm or discomfort earlier produces some anxiety. Just remembering the discomfort brought on the anxiety.

We are all aware of the separation anxiety we felt when we went off to school or summer camp or college. We were anxious because we were not sure what the new experience would bring. We did not know what we had and how to function in it. The same would be true regarding death. Our anxiety would be the fear of not knowing what was going to happen next, or how we would cope. Questions arise at funerals that indicate that, perhaps for the first time, people are asking about life after death, the nature of God, and who and what they are compared to other forms of existence. Death does make us pause to contemplate, and, in that contemplation, feel anxious about not only the person who died but about also about ourselves and what might become of us.

Though emptiness, guilt, and anger are dynamics of grief, it does seem clear that anxiety is prevalent throughout our struggle with grief.

All of you have no doubt become aware of one author or another's concept of the stages of grief. Some twenty-five years ago, Elizabeth Kubler-Ross wrote a book called *On Death and Dying*. It began a more open and frank discussion about death, preparing for death, and dealing with the death of a loved one than any work I have seen since. There have been many other authors who have suggested similar "stages" of death and dying. I was fortunate to hear a lecture by Dr. Alan Wolfelt, who directs the Center for Loss and Life

Transition, on this topic. He identified three stages of grief. The first was what he called the "evasion of the new reality." In this stage, the person goes through the normal reactions to death: shock, denial, numbness. The normal reactions tend to help us protect ourselves against the horrible shock of accepting that one we knew and loved is dead. I have seen many parishioners go through this stage of grief. I have been by their side as they watched their mate die. In long-term care facilities, most often one spouse has already died before the survivor comes to the assisted-living community or nursing home, but sometimes we are fortunate to have couples living together or to have single people find each other and marry within the building. I had one couple in my last facility that planned to move in together. The man came to see the facility and made the arrangements because his wife was in the hospital and would need nursing attention when she got out. The day after they moved in, he died. His wife was quite upset. She had just lost her house, her independence, her health, and now her husband. She went through the shock, the denial, and the numbness. Everyone thought she was handling the situation well, but she was just going through the motions. After the funeral, she said, "I bet he's waiting for me back at the home." At this point, clergy can be helpful at addressing the reality of the situation without slapping people across the face. Visiting the resident and sending lay friends to visit can be very helpful. Encourage the other parishioners to send sympathy cards. The best thing we can do is to simply be there when the shock wears off, the denial is over, and the reality sets in.

The second stage Dr. Wolfelt identifies is called "encounter with new reality." Here people become anxious, panic, and are fearful because they are beginning to realize what the death will mean for their own lives. One might express explosive emotions or be irrational in blaming themselves. They may feel guilt, remorse, loss, emptiness, or sadness. In the facility where I now work, there is a lady whose husband died. She got through the first stage of shock and denial, but then she began to blame herself for his death because she allowed him to eat fatty foods and to sit around rather than exercise in any way. She was the classic "turtle" that blamed herself for his ill health. This is the time when questions about eternal life come up. The questions may be regarding the deceased but may also be asked as a way of reassuring oneself.

In the final stage, Dr. Wolfelt indicates that "reconciliation to the new reality" takes place. In this stage, one may feel some relief, or release; a sense of letting go. Finally there is reconciliation, acceptance. Most people get to this point. We have memorial services when a resident dies in our facility as a way of helping the residents there who could not get to the normal funeral service. At the last one, I said to those gathered that in spite of our loss of a friend, our lives must go on. I alluded to the resident whose husband had died just after they moved in. The wife was doing fine after two years. I used her as an example. Sure she missed her husband, but life goes on and so did she. Visits to the facility to listen to the thoughts and fears of going on alone are a good way to minister to those who have gone through the shock and anxiety associated with grief.

Reconciliation is a process that takes time. It is not an event that occurs suddenly. How long it takes for someone to move to the point of reconciliation is unique for each person. Special occasions like holidays, anniversaries, and birthdays may trigger a resurgence of feelings that the person thought they had worked through. There are, I believe, some things we must do before we can move to final reconciliation. First of all, we must accept the finality of our loss. A couple becomes a single. One's life mate is gone. They are not away on a trip, but gone. It is a hard first step. Second, our lives must begin to return to normal. Our normal sleeping and eating habits must return to what they had been. But the one we had shared our beds with and our meals with will not be there. The transition is difficult. Next, we must feel a sense of release, knowing that the worst of the hurt is over and we are moving on. Some will have guilty feelings when they realize they are hurting less, as if the expectations of society were for them to mourn forever. Eventually, one must begin to enjoy him or herself. Oftentimes churches have an older adult singles group that meet for fellowship. To be finally reconciled, we must begin to live again, to move away from the grave and back into life. Perhaps the next step is most indicative of progress. We must begin to plan for the future and not continue to live in the past. Finally, we must be open to the many changes that are sure to occur.

I am sure that you have seen people who have gotten stuck at one of these points and have not become fully reconciled to the death of their spouse. I remember a lady in a former church who insisted that she be referred to as Mrs. Harold _____. She had not moved past feeling a sense of release. She certainly did not enjoy life. Most of my conversations with her were about the past. She seemed to have no joy. There was seldom any mention of future plans. She was stuck, and I am not sure if she has ever come to final reconciliation.

I mentioned earlier that the second dynamic of grief was fear. I bring it up at this point to highlight something I have noticed over the years. I believe that most of us have a fear of death. It is a fear that has its roots in the very nature of our being as a finite creature. The death of someone near to us tends to personalize death and stimulate the fear of our own impending death. This makes it difficult to discuss it or plan for it. Many people avoid preparing wills for this reason. Just talking about one's death is frightening. When someone we know dies, we begin to think about when our "time will come."

From my early childhood, I have been aware of something "spooky" about death. Ghosts, spirits, bodies rising, cemeteries, funeral homes, all were put into the category of things to fear. When someone is dead, there is something distinctly different about him or her. They are not "normal" and for that reason there is a fear, a fear of the unknown, a fear of the dead body. Many generations ago in some parts of our country, the custom upon the death of a family member was to have the body for "viewing" in the parlor or living room of their house. People were selected to sit up with the deceased all night. I believe that part of the reason for this ritual was to ensure the safety of the family. There is indeed an element of fear involved in our understanding of death.

A third kind of fear we find mixed up in the emotions of death is the fear of our own suffering. Not all relationships are always smooth. If someone dies before we can share our true feelings with them, or bring about reconciliation, we suffer anxiety and guilt for not being more kind, loving, considerate, willing to compromise, etc. Perhaps the old adage of not going to bed angry with someone has merit to it! Or better yet, perhaps we should live in such a way as not to make enemies.

My final observation about death and fear is that oftentimes when someone dies, we look at ourselves and say, "Now what am I going to do?" I have heard it many times from widows asked in many different ways. They may feel abandoned by the spouse who has died. In past generations, oftentimes the role of the husband and wife was clearly defined. When one died, the other was ill prepared to assume the duties once handled by the deceased. There was a clear sense, a fear, of being unable to do all that was now required.

Once again we find ourselves at the point of asking, "What can we do for those who grieve?" The image of the pastor is one that exemplifies, among other symbols, the spirit of Him who came to comfort and to heal broken relationships. Most often, the minister can communicate the concern of the god whom he serves, the church he represents, and the community in which he lives. The pastor can symbolize, just by his or her presence, that God does not forsake. Imagine how important it is to be with a family when a loved one dies. In the midst of their anger, fear, and anxiety, the pastor serves as a symbol of hope, even without saying a word!

The role of the minister in the therapy of bereavement will be proportionate to the relationship he or she had previously established prior to the death and the grief. The better we know our congregation, the better we can minister to them in this very difficult time. The day I moved from my seminary apartment to my first church, I met a lady who was waiting for me on the front porch of the parsonage. Her husband had died earlier that day. How effective do you think I was at the funeral and afterwards as this lady dealt with her grief? Not knowing the person who died or the family made the funeral and comments made there seem hollow and to have little impact. For this and many other reasons, it is so important to share "pastoral" responsibilities with members of the congregation. They can be an asset to the pastor as well as to the church member.

Just knowing the parishioner may not be the answer to effective pastoral care, especially if the pastor is not comfortable with his own understanding of death and dying. But officiating at a few funerals will soon compel the pastor to ask him or herself some hard questions. Death, even for a minister, is a certain undeniable fact, compelling choices of either hope or despair. The mystery, the burden of knowing one has to die, is a fact of existence. Existentialists tell us that the greatest threat experienced is the threat of "angst," the threat of non-being, hence, death. The minister's own view of death or his remembrance of poignant grief can become carried over into the relationship with the grief sufferer. This emotional freight will color his feelings, thinking, and actions.

To minister to the grief sufferer, the pastor or specially trained laity must be supportive without doing the grief work for the family. They must enable the sufferer to tell of his loss, his story in his own way and in his own words. As the story of the events prior to the death is told over and over again, it has a cathartic effect upon the teller. It becomes easier to tell and thus easier to bear. The sufferer needs those who will listen with deep and abiding concern, who will empathize with them.

When we consider that most people over age sixty-five have experienced the death of a grandparent, and perhaps a parent, they are candidates to not only experience yet another death, that of a parent or spouse, but also that they are the people in the congregation who could be best able to empathize with others who mourn. I have mentioned many times how laity can be very effective in providing pastoral care. There is no doubt that this is an especially good way to involve the older church member. It is not too strenuous or physically demanding. It does not require night driving, but allows the older member the opportunity to minister at his or her own pace. So long as people are able to listen rather than retell there own grief story, they can be very effective.

Ministering to laity with laity is a fine way of involving the elderly, but it should not take the place of pastoral involvement. Pastoral counseling is a difficult and demanding discipline. It involves a one-to-one relationship in which the pastor and the church member work toward the solution or resolution of a problem. The pastor must allow the individual to grow at their own rate at the level of their own need. You will find that the person suffering the pain of loss needs individual attention in direct proportion to the situation. The loss sufferer needs the support of someone outside of the family but inside the family of God to hear his or her cries and offer hope.

In my second church, I had a family that was not very active. They had a boat and spent many of their weekends on the river. One day, the husband and his brother were racing in the boats and ended up going over a lock, killing all but one of the people in the two boats. The mother survived, but her husband and three children along with her brother-in-law and his family all died. The amount of time required to assist this woman through her grief was tremendous. She was not eating, not sleeping, and unable to function for the longest time. But little by little, she was able to move on.

I have found that the pastoral tools most effective in grief support are: genuine love for others, sensitivity to others, and listening. Disciplined listening encourages others to talk. This is very important in the early stages of grief. Responsive listening where the pastor responds to what the person is saying, hearing the meaning behind the words, catching the nuances and overtones, becomes effective as the grief sufferer begins to express feelings. Both these kinds of listening are important as they are incorporated into an atmosphere of permissive counseling. It is usually best to have a church member come to the study or office for counseling because it is not home where they may need to feel like they are the host or hostess. It is also a good idea to have Kleenex handy because in that intimate space where no one else is around, oftentimes people open up and emotions flow.

Chapter Eight
Faith Development and
Spirituality

*Unlike our bodies, our faith continues to grow
stronger the longer we live.*

In this chapter I would like to look at the issues of faith development, spirituality, religious significance, and the primary needs of the older adult. This overview will help better understand concerns that the post-retirement age has regarding their lives and the faith.

I begin this overview with some assistance from Erik Erikson. Mr. Erikson wrote a book that was published in 1963. It was called *Childhood and Society* and has become a standard for educators. A follow-up book written in 1968 is called *Identity Youth and Crisis*. Both these books contain what has become a standard in understanding people from childhood through adulthood. Erickson's emphasis is on the children and youth, but he does add insight into the stages we all go through in our lives. I quote from his *Identity Youth and Crisis* book but both contain what is commonly known as the "Life Cycle." This cycle has within it eight stages of ego development. The stage of interest to us is the final one wherein Erikson discusses the issue of integrity versus despair. If one has been successful in moving through the previous seven stages, dealing with intimacy, adapting to triumphs and disappointments, meeting vocational goals, and helping to create some positive social change, then he is ready to deal with looking back over his life and accepting responsibility for what has been accomplished. Integrity, says Erikson, is "the ego's accrued assurance of its proclivity for order and meaning—an emotional integration faithful to the image-bearers of the past and ready to take, and eventually to renounce, leadership in the present. It is the acceptance of one's one and only life cycle and of the people who have become significant to it as something that had to be and that, by necessity, permitted of no substitutions."[18] The lack of or even the loss of this accrued ego integration is signified by despair. A definition once again from Erikson says that despair expresses the feeling that time is short, too short for the attempt to start another life and to try out alternate roads to integrity.[19] For the elderly then, this final stage is a time to look back over their lives and to feel comfortable with their accomplishments, accepting what they have become as their own, or a time to fret because they have not done so and it is too late to make amends. Understanding this stage and those that came before it can help explain why some older adults have such a hard time as they age. Those with estranged families, with no friends, or who seem bitter and angry have not been successful in completing this stage of ego development, and may not have been successful at others either. It would be worth another

---

[18]   Erick Erickson, *Identity Youth and Crisis* (New York: W.W. Norton Company, 1968), 139.

[19]   Ibid., 140.

look at either of Erikson's books I have cited to learn more about ego development.

Some years ago, James Fowler wrote a book on faith development. In it he identified six stages of faith development that seem to have correlation with the age and emotional development as set forth by Erik Erikson. I would like to examine the final two stages of faith development, wherein I believe most of our adult church members find themselves.

Stage four in Fowler's understanding of faith development is called the "Individuative-Reflective Faith." Most often people enter this stage as young adults, but many people never move beyond it. This stage of our faith development is a struggle for most of us. In it, we are torn between individuality and being defined by a particular group. When we were younger, we did what our parents told us. We went to worship where they went to worship and when they went to worship, but as young adults we went off to college or to the military or got married and began a life of our own. At some point we either accepted for ourselves what our parents had imposed upon us or we chose to go our own way. That is why we so often find young adults as inactive members of the church. At some point, usually with marriage, the birth of children, or some dramatic event, the young adult either picks up where he or she was or grows into the next stage, where their identity is no longer defined by the composite of one's roles or meanings to others. Belief is personal, not corporate, decided upon after reflection and a new understanding of self.

Oftentimes, people who are living in this stage of faith development are able to translate symbols into conceptual meanings. The cross takes on a new meaning that is personal. The Eucharist becomes more than bread and cup. Jesus is bigger than the picture on the wall.

Fowler identifies the strength of this stage with the ability to reflect critically on who we are and also on what we believe. The young person who inspires and leads others has come to this point. They find out who they are and they identify clearly what they believe. For those who are still struggling to find out who they are and what they believe, this person can be a leader, a revolutionary. The danger of this stage is in thinking that now, finally, one has all the answers![20]

Many adults stay in this fourth stage of faith development. It is comfortable. It is personal. It makes sense for many. But there are others who, through exploration of or exposure to other denominations or religions, begin to feel uneasy. Answers to questions like why bad things happen to good people begin to shake what was once a firm personal belief. Tragedies like the death of a child, spouse, or parent can make any of us question what we believe. For some, these tragedies and the recognition that life is more complex than one once believed compel them to move ahead with their faith development.

---

[20] James Fowler, *Stages of Faith: The Psychology of Human Development and the Quest for Meaning* (San Francisco: Harpercollins, College Division, 1981), 182-187.

Fowler calls this next stage of faith development "conjunctive faith." This kind of faith involves the reclaiming and reworking of one's past. People at this stage become more open to their deeper self, their real self, not the shallow self or the masked self that is projected for the benefit of others. This may involve a critical recognition of our social unconscious. Neighbor is broadened, and concern for the plight of others is heightened. Church affiliation is less important than meeting the needs of others. The person in this stage may be very active in the church, but may also give money and time to other organizations who are meeting the social needs better than the church. They are the mission-minded people who see ministry to the poor as more important than building new buildings. The examination of oneself at this stage may mean examining the social myths and prejudices that we have allowed to be a part of who we have been for years. Whereas, in stage four, people struggled to clarify, in terms of boundaries of self and outlook, in this stage, those same boundaries become porous and permeable. In this stage, one seeks similarity and unity for a greater goal. The people who are at this level are more open to the truths of others. They no longer have to have the right answer to life's questions, but are open to hearing from others. Those who live in this stage have a commitment to justice that goes beyond what the family, community, church, or nation hold as just. They are able to see issues from many perspectives and not only one. Sometimes their actions seem to make no sense to others because they are no longer bound by doing what "society" says is correct. They answer to a "higher authority" and are willing to go to jail or be ostracized by others.

The strength that Fowler identifies in this "conjunctive faith" stage comes in the rise of ironic imagination. In this stage, the person is able to see and understand the most powerful meanings in life while also recognizing that those very meanings are relative.[21]

Because this stage of faith development is so late in life, those who are fortunate to enter it have also had some of the misfortunes of life. They have seen defeat and failure. They have experienced loss. They have made mistakes, some of which they cannot undo. Alive to paradox and the truth in apparent contradiction, this stage strives to unify opposites in mind and experience. It generates and maintains vulnerability to the strange truths of those who are different from them. This stage finds people ready for closeness to that which is different and threatening including new depths of experience in spirituality and religious revelations. One is freed, perhaps by age, perhaps by a mature faith, to get beyond what the community, culture, race, religious community, or even country holds most high. The seriousness that can arise when life is more than half over enables people in this stage to be ready to give themselves to the cause of enabling others to generate identity and meaning in their lives.

Our church members in this stage would say things like, "I guess it doesn't matter what church you belong to, so long as you believe." They would get beyond the

---

[21]   Ibid., 186-198.

confines of one denomination or even one religion as the one holding the whole truth to knowing God.

Those who are in long-term care facilities have experienced the traumas of aging, the losses that go hand in hand with getting old and giving up their homes, and are often better prepared to function as a person who gets beyond the bounds of denomination or even organized religion. Their faith is personal and developed through the struggles of life.

The sixth stage, "universalizing faith," is very rare. The person best described by it has generated faith compositions in which their felt sense of an ultimate environment is inclusive of all being. They have become incarnators and actualizers of the spirit of an inclusive and fulfilled human community. There are no boundaries. Their community is universal in extent. They have gone beyond what most of us can ever imagine in their faith development.[22]

When we look at this age outside of faith development, we find that people in the older adult age group are trying to simplify their lives, unburden themselves of the responsibilities of trying to earn a living, competing to get ahead in their jobs. At the same time, people of this age try to maintain a sense of worth and significance. They want to and deserve to be treated as the elders in the family, the church,

---

[22] Ibid., 200.

and the community. In this, we have failed as a church. We have not shown to our elders the respect and honor they deserve. Some of us find it hard to listen to their reason when we are not as mature in our faith as are they. We may want sticks and bricks, when they are calling for loaves and fishes. We may want church loyalty and identity, while they support ministries and missions of various kinds.

I remember visiting one of the shut-ins in the second church I served. She gave me her pledge card to return to the church with some explanation. She told me that since she could not get out to worship, she watched one of the ministers on television. She was going to split her tithe between the local church and the TV minister. I was a little surprised and even more surprised with my response. I asked her when that minister had given her communion last or visited her in the hospital. I asked if he was going to preside at her funeral service. Unfortunately, I lacked any measure of good sense or compassion. My shut-in was concerned about her church, but she had found other ways to help people like herself who might never come into a church building.

It seems like these senior adult years are especially difficult for many reasons. The older adult experiences changes of a wide variety from retirement to death of spouse to loss of esteem to physical debilitation to life in an institution. They are forced to adjust to these and many more changes as their lives progress from retirement onward. At some point, the children start paying for dinner and assuming more of a leadership role in the family. They will make some decisions on behalf of the parent. Decisions like taking away the driver's license, selling the car, and going into a retirement community are usually made on behalf of the parent, for the good of everyone. It is very difficult for the senior to accept the new roles in which they find themselves. It seems like they have to come to terms with many issues like illnesses and declining health. These issues are of major importance because they usually impact the rest of their lives. What I have seen of these struggles indicates to me that going through teen-age years is a breeze compared to becoming an older adult. How do we help them during these trying times? What support do we offer? Is there a way for those who have experienced similar problems to help ease the pain of those who are currently under stress?

The primary needs of people in this age group seem obvious. They need help facing the major decisions, dealing with the losses and accepting the situation as it is. But perhaps more importantly, they need help discovering meaning in what they see happening to them. They have to see purpose and worth for their lives. But the older people get and the more infirmed they become, the more difficult it is to see anything but more losses until ultimately there is loss of life itself. Can we, as pastors, not provide them with some hope to support them during these trying times?

I remember seeing a movie many years ago about an older woman who was a widow. She was somewhat active in her retirement home. She got visits from family and neighbors. Life on the outside seemed okay, but what we learned that she lacked was a relationship with someone who called her by her first name. She wanted a relationship with someone who was close enough to her emotionally to call her by the first name. As spouses and friends die, oftentimes what is left for our older adults are people who know them but do not really know them. How lonely that must be.

It is interesting to see the people in this age group as they talk about and prepare for death. Some are quite open and talk about funeral plans, do not resuscitate orders, the desire to "go home to Jesus." Others are in no big hurry. Some people are what my father calls "sour"; they are the people who seem to never be happy and whose goal it seems is to make those around them sad as well. I believe that some of this behavior has to do with whether or not they have come to grips with their lives. Confronted so often by signs of aging and death, they are afforded many opportunities to look back over their lives and assess how they have been. There may be opportunities to makes things right or to offer apologies or forgiveness. Some have their spiritual houses in order and are emotionally ready for when they will be among us no longer. Others are not ready. They may not be willing to make any necessary changes or to offer forgiveness to restore a relationship. Timely sermons that deal with these issues can help nudge some of the older church members into "doing the right thing."

It seems that religious perspectives on aging originate in a paradox: We somehow experience growth as we decline. Religious traditions are able to reconcile this paradox by looking at loss as fertile ground in which spiritual life can grow and blossom. The many losses associated with age catalyze the beginning of what is seen as a spiritually rich time of life. The normal conditions of later life, of old age, oftentimes bring a renewed urgency to the spiritual quest. The events common in later life may be viewed as an invitation to meet with particular vitality the spiritual challenges of aging. These challenges encourage the elderly to look inward, to evaluate their relationships and the choices they have made and eventually, and to come to terms with what was and what is in their lives.

I believe that the major world religions all point to late life as an honorable phase of the life cycle that presents distinct opportunities for spiritual growth and involvement within the religious community.

The elderly can take stock and reexamine and shape new meanings from a whole life for the benefit of themselves and others. Many world religions see the older years as a time for contemplation. As individuals age, the roles and responsibilities of work and family diminish, freeing them to give more attention to the questions of meaning, purpose, and the work of integration.

What a person believes dictates how he will act. If we are sure of our salvation and are certain that eternal life will be ours, we will face the end of our lives with courage. You have no doubt heard the stories of people who, while facing certain death for their testimony, have witnessed to their faith. Not everyone will have this opportunity, but all of us do know for certain that we will face death. As we age, the certainty of our death becomes more eminent. Spouses and friends die. Health declines. We are unable to do all the things we would like. At this point, the elderly experience some anxiety about their future. No matter how strong our faith, it is natural to be concerned. How can the church help people with this kind of anxiety? How can we allow each other to be honest with our doubt or fear? Shaming people into displaying a strong faith is not the answer. What ways can we allow others to talk about their unbelief? How can we enable them to grow stronger? What kind of reassurance can we give to allow them to express doubt while at the same time being faithful? The answers to these questions I believe depend on the relationship of the clergy to the older adult. When visits are made to shut-ins or people in long-term care facilities, time must be taken to inquire about more than health. Time must be given to allow the older church member to express doubts or concerns. Perhaps by talking about a fellow church member who has died, pastors can open up conversation about faith or hope. By asking what they think about varying theological perspectives, we can encourage a discussion that moves away from the rather trite responses we may otherwise get. But this kind of discussion takes time, and it means that we must pay attention to answers. We can provide no better service than to help those who struggle with their faith find some answers that make sense to them, that will enable them to close their eyes at night in the sure hope of salvation.

I would like to conclude this chapter with some comments about faith and spirituality as they relate to the demented. Obviously the term covers people with many different abilities and needs, but let me talk for a moment in generalities that may help in specific situations. Remembering my earlier definition, those who are demented have suffered some sort of trauma to their brain that creates loss of memory and poor judgment, which may result in inappropriate actions or behavior. With Alzheimer's disease, the victim continues to lose memory and abilities to function even to the point of recalling family members, how to walk, and how to shallow. What they do recall about their faith and religious life also diminishes along with other memory. At an early stage, they may be able to participate in worship with their family. They may lose the ability to read music and only sing along with the old songs. Gradually, only the songs they learned as a child will be recalled. And eventually, when speech is affected, they may only be able to hum old tunes. What is true of music is also true of scripture. As we age we hear and learn more scripture. We have heard sermons on some of them many times. The popular ones will be recalled. But as memory is destroyed, scripture learned late in life will be destroyed with it. What remains is scripture learned early in life. What do we teach our children in Sunday school? Most often they learn stories like Noah and the ark, and Moses as a child and later parting the waters and giving the Ten Commandments. They learn about the heroes of the faith, David, Jonah, Jesus, Nicodemus, Peter, and Paul. The Christmas stories of the wise men and the shepherds are of major importance due to the pageantry that often goes with them. (I remember being a wise man with my two brothers.) They learn the stories of struggle and faith. These stories remain until they too are lost. But while they remain, they are affirmed and still held as they were when first learned, as examples for the faithful. The point to be made is that those who suffer a continual loss of memory, such as those who have Alzheimer's disease, can be touched spiritually at the level of their recall. They cannot learn more scripture or become more advanced in their faith. It is the job of the pastor to minister to their needs at the level where they exist.

When I do devotions in the "special needs" unit of the facility where I work, I choose a scripture that I am sure the residents will know. I read it and then try to relate it to their lives at the moment. We pray for families, our neighbors, and repeat the twenty-third Psalm or pray the Lord's Prayer. We may sing the first verse of a song like "The Old Rugged Cross" or "Amazing Grace." Not everyone can sing or say all the words, but most of the residents can. The devotional time that is simple and short is best.

As people with Alzheimer's continue to lose memory and other abilities, they may still be able to be touched spiritually with music and symbolism. The old music they learned as children may still strike a chord. One of the first songs we learn that is also the cornerstone of our faith is "Jesus Loves Me." The song and the sentiment serve us well for many years and are an example of what is simple and basic but also lasting and substantial in our faith development. The symbol of a Bible or a cross may draw the demented adult toward memories of worship and Bible verses. And in the end, that may be all they are able to take in or recall.

Understanding faith development will help pastors do a better job in worship and as a pastor to the person in need. Understanding the cognitive deficiencies of a demented adult will enable the minister to reach the parishioner at a point where he may understand and respond. Taking the time to understand will serve the minister well as he or she serves the older members of the congregation.

Ministry to and with the Elderly

Chapter Nine
Long-Term Care Facility Worship

Old voices still sing!

The area of ministering to and with the elderly where I have seen the greatest need is when clergy come to the long-term care facilities to provide a worship service. I would like to talk about how to conduct worship in a long-term care facility when you have been asked to be the visiting pastor.

The most important thing to remember is that those who are living in these facilities are the aged or very old according to an earlier definition. Their bodies and senses are failing. A stroke or a disease may have affected their memory or even ability to speak. The worship, therefore, should be brief, using familiar songs, scripture verses, and prayers.

I mentioned before how important light is to the aging eye. A simple experiment to enable you to know how an older person may be seeing things could be to use some yellow film wrap over glasses to represent the color older people see. The second is to smear Vaseline on glasses and try to see through them. These tests will help you see how much light is too much or too little. If you expect the people in the facility to read, be sure there is enough light.

A second thing that seems common to the aged is the loss of hearing. Do not be shy. Speak up. No matter how big a voice you think you have, use amplification if it is available, and if not project so that you are comfortable that everyone hears you. It is easy to tune out or doze off during worship if you can't hear what is being said. Again, try the cotton in the ears experiment to remind yourself how loudly you must speak to be heard by all.

We recently had a worship service in one of the buildings I currently serve. I had the amplification system on and opened the service by introducing the guest minister. He decided to move out from behind the lectern because the space was not all that large and he assumed he could be heard. After just a few minutes, one of the residents stood up and began to leave. I approached her and asked if she was okay. Her response was that she was fine, but that she could not understand what the minister was saying so she might as well leave.

Remember that not everyone is able to kneel or even stand up. Try to structure your service so that it does not require these things. I remember watching people as they struggled to rise one day when an insensitive minister was conducting worship and asked everyone to rise as the scripture was being read. Most long-term care facilities are sensitive to the needs of the elderly by providing chairs with arms that enable people to push themselves up, but this is not easy for some people. Many of the people in attendance will not be able to stand without the help of a nurse. Some will not be able to stand at all. Stroke victims may be able to stand on only one leg. Some will sit in their wheelchairs and not be able to do much else. People who have had legs amputated as a result of diabetes would not only not be able to stand, but would feel uncomfortable because their disability was once again painfully obvious.

I was a speaker recently before a group of pastors who served as chaplains in nursing homes and assisted-living facilities. The question raised from that group was "How do we include everyone in worship?" I answered the question by asking the group to imagine that they had one ailment or disease at time and talked about how even the person who cannot see or hear may be able to taste and, therefore, become aware of a spiritual event when communion is served.

Let me give some brief examples. If someone is having difficulty seeing, be sure the bulletins are in large print. I recommend that bulletins be printed using at least a fourteen-point font. Turn on as much light as possible. (Forget about atmosphere.) If someone has poor eyesight and is hard of hearing, ask them to sit up front near the speaker. If they are deaf, perhaps tapping them on the shoulder softly as you sing and seating them next to the organ or piano would be helpful. If they are deaf but can still see, the symbols of the cross, the Bible, and the communion cup are visual cues that will enable them to understand what is happening. Consider preparing your message ahead of time and having it for the deaf person to read as you preach it to the rest of the residents gathered. Because so many of the people are wheelchair bound, don't ask them to stand. As mentioned earlier, not everyone is able to do this, and it only serves to draw attention to those who are infirm in this way. For those who are demented, who may speak out, be reassuring and make the service simple. Those with dementia can often remember the old music and prayers they learned as a child. Use these.

I relayed the story earlier of the lady in my first facility that was a stroke victim. She could not speak. One day, we were in worship, singing an old, familiar hymn, when she began to sing. When the song ended, tears streamed down her face, but when she tried to speak she could not. The words from the old song were stored somewhere in her mind that was not affected by the stroke. She could really sing! What a fine example of a joyful noise!

If someone happens to be deaf and blind, they may still recognize the taste of the host and the cup during communion. Even if you take it to them in their room, these elements of communion will enable the resident (parishioner) to feel like they have been a part of a worship setting. Someone who is deaf or blind may still be able to smell. If your tradition has been to use incense in worship, the smell of burning incense alone may help people realize that they are in a worship setting. Do not overlook flowers. I'm not sure where that tradition came from, but most churches have flowers on the altar or communion table for worship. Ask whoever donated them if you can use them in this setting as well, or, even better, ask another church member if they would give you some flowers from their yard or garden that you can take. Flowers normally have an aroma that once again points to the majesty of a creative God. Use whatever senses the resident has at his disposal to enable him to once again come to God through worship.

I'm sure there are many others ways to enable the institutionalized parishioner to enjoy a modified version of worship. Participation will be limited only by one's disability, but even that can be overcome with some forethought and planning.

Be sure to enable those who are living in long-term care facilities to participate in worship. Many of these folks are former ushers who love to hand out the bulletins and straighten up after worship is concluded. These folks are oftentimes the outgoing type of people who enjoy greeting others as they come to worship. Be sure to find someone who can do this and would like to assume that role when you visit. Nearly every facility has a piano. If you do not have someone who can go with you to play the hymns, ask if there is someone at the facility who can play. Once again, if you select the old hymns, chances are you may find someone who would be willing to play a few hymns in worship. Just as it is possible in most cases to find a piano player, you may also find someone who can sing a special song as a means of praising God. In fact, most choirs in local churches have older people in them. This would be a good opportunity for one older person to be in ministry to another. If there are no older choir members available, perhaps someone at the facility would like to sing. People who are older are still able to sing, and would probably like the chance to do so in front of their new friends. If you are going to serve the Eucharist, you may need some assistance setting up. You may need to find someone who cannot sing to hand out bulletins or play the piano or set up the cups or bread. There are many ways even the very old can be in ministry to one another in worship in a facility.

My grandfather was a Roman Catholic. As he grew older, he moved within walking distance of his church. He had always been an early riser and enjoyed going to Mass first thing each day. He discovered that the priest often did not have an altar boy to assist him for the 6:00 a.m. Mass, so he volunteered. He must surely have been the oldest altar boy in the diocese.

I recall from my days as a parish minister that providing worship at the local nursing home was not very high on my list of important things to do. Hospital visits, visits in the homes, funerals, counseling sessions, and even meetings took precedent. Taking time to prepare for a half-hour service seemed like it was always put off to the last minute. Many times I would ignore the advice of my homiletics professor and simply pull out an old sermon to preach. But when I did this, I always walked away feeling like those who were at the facility had been shortchanged. I was right. If anything, it takes more time to prepare for this kind of worship than it does to prepare for a normal worship service. Consideration must always be made for the audience. Not only must we consider their physical and mental conditions, but also we must remember that illustrations need to be appropriate. This part of preaching to the elderly is most difficult for the younger pastor. Perhaps it would be good to ask some older church members if they can think of examples or stories that may help illustrate a point. By involving others, they too become a part of this ministry to the elderly. In fact, it is another illustration of how some older members can help minister to others. Worship preparation for long-term care facilities, when done with integrity, takes time and effort.

Let me share one final comment regarding worship in long-term care facilities. If you have a parishioner living in one of these facilities, let them know you are coming. They talk about the fact that their "preacher" is going to lead worship. Their anticipation gives them something to talk about, and, if you do a good job, something to brag about! Most people living in these kinds of facilities have lived in the same area for some time. They know the history of each others' churches and may have been in them for weddings or funerals. They remember and talk about the clergy and special events in their lives when the church meant so much to them. *Never* underestimate the importance of your ministry to these people.

I was asked to speak at a worship service at a retirement community where we had about a dozen members living. One lady asked my family and me to be her guests for dinner prior to the evening service. The way we were received by this lady and the other residents made me feel like I was king of the world. A special dining area was set up for all the church members, and I was placed at the head of the table. There was such love, support, and appreciation expressed there that I'm sure I did a better job in the service that followed than I had done on other occasions. It became clear to me how important my visit was to these people. Needless to say, I was always happy to be asked to lead worship there when my turn came around.

Worship in long-term care facilities is a vital part of life in these communities. It should also be an important part of every local church ministry. It takes time. It takes effort. It is essential in providing pastoral care because through worship wavering faith is restored, good news is shared, fellowship is created, and the love of God expressed in words, song, smiles, and hugs.

Chapter Ten
Programs

I have offered many program suggestions in each of the preceding chapters. In this one, I would simply like to list them as well as others that would enable any congregation to better minister to and with the elderly.

One of the churches I have attended had a nurturing committee whose job it was to design programs to assist in the nurturing and care of the membership. There were three programs that came from that committee that were designed for the elderly members of the congregation. The first was one where a church member was assigned to visit a shut-in member for one year. He or she made periodic visits to chat with the shut-in, or they might take them a home-made treat, or perhaps assist them by picking up a few groceries. They are simply visitors. They require no special training, but the people chosen should be compassionate or the visits become a chore and not a treat for the shut-in or the other church member. The second program was similar but it involved only a phone call. In this program, people are assigned a shut-in to call each day to make sure they were all right. These calls can be very short. They are simply designed to be the first step in alerting police or emergency personnel to a suspected problem. The third program was one where one of our retired ministers visited with all the shut-ins who were in retirement homes or long-term care facilities. He visited them once every three months and took the

Eucharist to them. All three programs used volunteers, some of whom were older adults themselves.

In addition to these three programs for the elderly shut-ins of that congregation, we also have a Stephen's Ministry program, where some of the trained laity were appointed to provide pastoral support to the elderly. They served as a support to the pastor, not as a replacement. It is important that the "preacher" go to visit the older member of the church. I have heard on more than one occasion people complain that since they can no longer get out to worship, they seem to be forgotten. One lady told me that she had been a Sunday school teacher for forty years and had served on the administrative leadership committees and the pastoral relations committee. She had always given her tithe and then some. Since she became a shut-in, the minister had not been by to visit. She felt neglected and hurt. As an associate pastor in a former church, I was offended one day when a shut-in asked why the "preacher" could not come to see her himself instead of sending me. There were five clergy at that church, all ordained, but she wanted to see the senior minister. She deserved to see the senior minister once in a while. I would encourage you to be aware of the feelings of these elderly and not to let pastoral care slide down your priority list in your church.

Some congregations have a visiting nurse program where licensed nurses visit the elderly who may need assistance with medication administration or their blood pressure taken on a regular basis. Many elderly are diabetic. A visiting nurse could help with an Accu-

Check or could administer an appropriate dose of insulin.

A component of this visiting nurse program is a visiting caregiver who is not a licensed nurse but someone like a nurse's aide, or even someone who has the gift of love for the elderly, who will give a bath or make a meal or clean a house. Any of these acts of kindness will enable an older person to live on their own just a little longer. Nearly anyone, with a little training, can give a bath or help someone get dressed, do some laundry, prepare a meal, do a little housecleaning, help balance a checkbook or any number of things we all seem to take for granted. This kind of assistance is "hands-on" and can be very gratifying for the caregiver who provides this service of love.

Many churches have a Meals On Wheels program that serves hot meals to the elderly. This kind of program serves to provide good nutrition for those who are shut in. For many of these older church members, these meals serve as their primary source of food each day. Most programs run only five days a week, which means that over the weekend, many people make do with something simple they can prepare for themselves.

Those who provide these meals are oftentimes over sixty-five themselves. The drivers or delivery personnel are those who are home around noon each day. Those who just happen to fit this category are those most recently retired. They are still able-bodied and can drive or deliver the meals from the cars to the homes. Many times the best delivery person is the person who is very outgoing and enjoys talking to people. They can be upbeat and share a greeting with the shut-in.

Many churches use the meal delivery program to feed elderly in the community who are not members of their congregation but are in need of food. It is a good way to minister to all God's children. A brief message or scripture verse printed on a colorful piece of paper may be of inspiration to those who would otherwise not hear about God's love for them. Receiving the meals is a concrete example of that same love.

Drivers, runners, cooks, accountants, those who type the messages, and those who copy them all perform a ministry for the elderly. Many of those who do these tasks can and often are elderly themselves.

The church I served in Pittsburgh had an associate minister who brought to our congregation the concept of a social program for the elderly. They called themselves X.Y.Z., which stood for Extra Years of Zest. What a great idea. Their mission was primarily social. They had meals, went on outings, organized day trips, and had a wonderful time together. From that group came ideas for ministry to others who were unable to participate, and before long these older adults were finding ways to assist others in need. Their primary focus was to have fun, and that they did, but they ended up helping many others as well.

Adult day care is a program I have talked about at some length. Oftentimes, the person coming to this program is living with one of their children. Through this program, the older adult is served as well as the middle-aged son or daughter who may still be working. It provides activity, security, and nutrition to the older adult. It is also a good means of socialization for those who are left alone in their home or that of their children. The combination of adult and child day care programs makes wonderful sense. Those who are being ministered to are themselves ministering to others.

These day care programs are great opportunities for church members to be of assistance to one another. There no doubt are many people who could lead in some singing or crafts or meal preparation or dancing. Many others could show a video of their last trip and use it as a springboard for discussion. The opportunities are endless.

I served a church that had a wonderful program for membership care. One component of it was to organize the parish into "neighborhoods." Members who lived within a certain number of blocks were in the same "neighborhood" and were brought together occasionally for fellowship or other church-related events. The leader of the neighborhood checked on those in the neighborhood once a month. They were aware when families were having problems, when someone was ill, and when there were specific pastoral needs. When there was a death in their neighborhood, they contacted the church office as well as the others in the neighborhood. The shut-ins were of special concern to these neighborhood leaders. They called them more often and made an effort to involve them in the life of the church as much as possible.

Many churches use laity to take the consecrated elements of the Eucharist to the shut-ins. This service helps the shut-in members as well as the laity who are privileged to serve in this capacity. When they go to the home of the shut-in, the layperson usually takes an audiotape of the service so that the older member may participate as fully as possible. Sharing the elements is a very personal and very special. The layperson is afforded the opportunity to share the symbol of God's love like no other.

Oftentimes, there is no official program where rides are offered to the elderly who can no longer drive to worship. Programs that have been developed usually are developed geographically. People who live near or drive by an older member are asked to call ahead and then stop to pick up the older member. Many times we say to an older church member, "If you ever need anything, just call." Of course, the call never comes. I have talked to many older adults who say they just hate to be a burden to someone else. The answer is to pair a younger member with an older one and to encourage the younger one to call and offer a ride every time they come to worship or a fellowship event. A Sunday school member may be the person who provides the ride, or perhaps a member of the choir. The important point of this program is to have the younger person be the one to initiate the calls, not the older adult.

It has become popular over the past ten years for churches to buy vans. They use the vans for youth work or to pick up children for Sunday school or vacation Bible school. They can also pick up the older adult who does not drive. Some of these vans are handicapped accessible with a wheelchair lift. This kind of van enables those who are wheelchair bound or who use electric scooters to be securely lifted into the van for transport. The person who drives the van will benefit from the service they provide. The wheelchair bound person will benefit from feeling as if they are still an active part of the congregation.

Large-print literature is an easy service we can offer to our older church members. The trick is to offer the large-print version in such a way as to not offend anyone. I have simply found it best to print things I want everyone to be able to read a little larger. Bulletins and devotional material should be offered in both large and small print. Large-print Bibles should be available in the older adult Sunday school classes, and large-print books should be available in the church library. The monthly newsletters that are mailed out should also be of large enough print to enable all our parishioners to read them. Church directories, minutes of the last meeting, and agendas all need to be printed so everyone can participate. Fund-raising literature is another area where the print may be too small. A general role of thumb is that nothing less than a fourteen-point font size should be used in materials you expect the older adult to be able to read.

In the program above, where I mentioned taking communion to the elderly, I mentioned taking audiotapes along to help them feel like they are a part of the service. It is important that we send audiotapes to our shut-ins weekly so that they can listen to it at their convenience. Many churches send videotapes out for their shut-ins to watch. Sending the large-print bulletin along also helps the shut-in feel as if they are participating rather than just listening or watching. It would be a good idea to also take along a large-print hymnal so they can read the rituals and sing the hymns.

Some churches have the advantage of broadcasting their worship services on television. This is ideal for those who cannot get out to worship. It would enhance their worship via the television broadcast to have the bulletins and hymnals that I mentioned above. These broadcasts are not only in the homes of local church members but also in every home, if they choose to watch. Perhaps the congregation could see this kind of broadcast as an evangelistic outreach to the unchurched or to all the homebound elderly in the community. Thinking ahead about who will potentially view the broadcast may help make it more enjoyable for all. An example may be printing the words to hymns so the viewer can see them to sing along. I even like the idea that some TV evangelists use of highlighting key phrases in writing as they bring up these points in their message. Those who have hearing problems may benefit from this small addition. Those who do not will have their worship enhanced by employing more than one medium of communication.

We can use TV for broadcasting things other than worship. I have found that churches in the southern part of the United States have far more adults in Sunday school than in the north. Most of the people who attend the class I attend have been going to it for years. It serves as a social as well as a spiritual center for our lives. Sometimes I get more out of it than I do out of worship! Why not televise an adult Sunday school class? Why not make it interactive so that class members who are shut in can call in questions for the teacher? Sunday school literature (large print) can be sent to the homes in preparation for the class. Phone line access that enables the viewer to hear the caller's questions or see it typed will enable everyone to participate in his or her classes, not simply sit and watch. There may be a local cable TV station studio that is not being used at 9:30 or 10:00 on Sunday morning. They will be equipped to take the calls and broadcast. Imagine how the elderly church member would feel to be able to continue to participate in a class they have been in for thirty years! What a ministry!

When using TV, the options are endless. Administrative meetings and annual meetings that may require votes can be televised to enable as many people as possible to participate. Of course, TV could be used for many other purposes other than enabling the shut-in to remain involved in the life of the church. There seems to be no limit other than our own imaginations.

Prayer lines or prayer chains are ways the elderly can feel like they are being in ministry to others. They can receive calls and pray for or on behalf of others at nearly any age. Some can do the calling to others, while others can do little more than pray. What could be more important?

As with any ministry in the church, it is important to try to discern the spiritual gifts of the elderly as they participate in ministry to one another. Dr. Charles Bryant, author of *Rediscovering Our Spiritual Gifts* and *Your Spiritual Gifts Inventory*, has identified thirty-two spiritual gifts. They are all biblical and represent the various gifts necessary for a church to continue to minister to the needs of the congregation and the community. He identified gifts like: prophecy, pastor, teaching, wisdom, knowledge, exhortation, discernment, giving, mercy, missionary, evangelism, hospitality, faith, leadership, administration, suffering, healing, prayer language, interpretation, intercessory prayer, martyrdom, service, spirit music, craftsmanship, exorcism, humor, miracles, and poverty. It would be good if all churches could identify the gifts of the congregation so that each person could use their God-given gift.

Is it possible to list all the members of the church who are "shut in?" This list could be placed in the bulletin or the newsletter with encouragement to pray for or visit them if possible. So often the shut-ins are simply forgotten. If this is not possible, how about listing their names when they are going to have a birthday? Everyone likes cards. I visited a shut-in once who had a least fifty cards all over her living room. They were birthday cards from her family and her church family. The cards had been up for two months!

Many churches have a church historian, but if not, how about a program where a younger person goes to visit the shut-ins with a tape recorder to record recollections of particular events such as a building campaign?

There are still some churches that have a group of women who quilt or sew to make lap robes for the people in wheelchairs. What a ministry it would be to set up classes where those who retain these skills can teach others who may have an interest but no one to teach them. One of my favorite gifts given to me by a church is a quilt that was made by the ladies of my smallest church. Many of these ladies had arthritis in their hands, but they enjoyed the company and worked until their discomfort got too much for them.

I mentioned before that it is quite certain that our older adults will experience grief during the years after retirement. Grief support is a program that would be of great assistance to them.

As much as we use the computer these days, it is clear that if the current church members who are over sixty-five do not use them, the next generation certainly will. I spoke recently with a dealer for Apple computers. He told me that in analyzing their sales history, he discovered that 62 percent of his sales had been to people over the age of fifty. Their primary desire to buy the computer was to have access to the Internet so they could keep in touch with children and grandchildren who no longer live nearby. The potential is certainly there. Can you imagine using e-mail for a special message to the older adults or a birthday greeting or even a prayer chain? Chat rooms could be set up for the older church members or for the church in general. Church Web pages could give up-to-date information on the needs of the parishioners that may enable the older adult to either get or give some kind of assistance. The possibilities for computer use are endless. A special committee of forward-thinking people familiar with computers and those aware of the needs of all church members, but especially the elderly, could propose opportunities for ministry that are endless.

The elderly have lived a lifetime and stand on the threshold of experience and wisdom and look back so as to offer guidance for future generations. Our attitudes do not help us to listen to their advice very often. We seldom take the time just to listen to older adults. They may not respond very quickly and may not be as rude as the rest of us; therefore, they wait until we are done speaking. We need to take the time to listen. How about a program where we teach church members to simply be good listeners? We all enjoy being heard. As people age they may lose a number of people around them with whom they can simply talk. What a treat it would be to have someone who asks a few questions about the past, present, or predictions for the future, who really is interested in what we have to say.

All these programs I have mentioned were or are attempts to minister to the needs of the elderly. Some enable the elderly person to be a source of comfort to others. There are many other ways to minister to and with the elderly. An older adult age level coordinator or special older adult ministry committee could be given the task of identifying needs and providing appropriate solutions. To use a phrase popular these days, we need to begin to think "outside the box" about our older adults, their abilities, and their needs.

Chapter Eleven
Agencies, Associations, and Helpful Organizations

I would like to briefly list some agencies or organizations that may also be of help to you as you seek to better understand the needs of the elderly and what is already available in most communities to meet those needs.

Area Agencies on Aging are government-funded agencies throughout the United States. They provide a variety of services such as transportation, case management, a meal program, senior centers, protective services, information and referral, and an ombudsman program.

Some of these agencies are called "senior services" of a particular area. Many times these services are provided at a reduced rate due to the government funding.

Adult day health care centers provide day care, socialization, supervision, food, structured activities, and medication distribution to the older adults who spend all of or a portion of the day in these centers. I mentioned that the last church I served had such a center. I would encourage you to investigate within your state what requirements there are for providing a similar service to your community.

American Association of Retired Persons is a well-known association that provides many services including insurance, pharmacy, financial, travel, and information. Its greatest influence on behalf of the elderly is political. Through the many chapters the association has throughout the country, it is able to quickly rally support by phone, letter, and e-mail for one particular bill or another at every level of government. It also offers support for the elderly and, of course, financial discounts in many businesses.

Case managers are a new profession of people who help families and individuals identify, coordinate, and monitor the community services a person needs as they age. They are aware of government services and regulations.

Durable medical equipment is sold by many different companies. This equipment is essentially assistive devices that help a person remain independent such as walkers, shower chairs, wheelchairs, canes, and motorized carts.

Elder law attorneys practice a particular kind of law that enables them to assist the elderly with will preparation, guardianship, power of attorney, living wills, help with taxes, assistance with Medicaid and Medicare benefits, and estate planning.

Home health care provides skilled nursing care and rehabilitative or therapeutic services including speech, occupational, and physical therapy in a person's home or in an assisted-living facility. Also included can be companionship, personal care, and homemaker services. These services provide non-medical assistance to persons whose physical conditions prevent their performance of routine personal tasks. Services many include assistance with bathing, dressing, light housekeeping, meal preparation, and grocery shopping. (I believe that our church members can provide these services to one another with some organization and a little training.)

The Lions Club is a service organization devoted to helping bring sight to the blind and hearing to the deaf. It raises money to provide free testing of sight and hearing and to provide glasses and hearing aids at a reduced rate.

Ombudsman programs are designed to assist our older adults who live in assisted-living or nursing facilities. They investigate complaints by the older adult or those made on their behalf.

Personal electronic response systems are electronic monitoring systems that allow a person to press a button worn around their neck in case they are unable to reach the phone in an emergency.

Protective services are usually a part of an Area Agency on Aging. They exist to investigate cases of suspected abuse, exploitation, abandonment, or neglect. They work in concert with other agencies to correct problems they find.

Respite care is in-home assistance allowing time off for family caregivers providing full-time care. This service can be provided by a home health agency. Many assisted-living facilities also offer this short-term stay of less than thirty days. Some associations offer financial assistance to families who are caring for their loved one that would enable them to pay for a home health aide to come into the home to allow them to get away for banking, shopping, or just to relax.

Senior assessment is a program that is often hospital based, where an assessment is made of the physical and mental conditions of an older person. By virtue of this assessment, appropriate services, medication, or placement can be suggested.

Senior centers are centers that offer a variety of services including socialization, meals, and educational programs.

Support groups are groups that have regularly scheduled meetings that provide members an opportunity to discuss their difficulties and learn coping or adaptive techniques. I have mentioned already how important and appropriate grief support can be in the setting of the church facility. It is also appropriate to open these facilities to other organizations that are seeking space such as the Alzheimer's Association or Heart Association.

The Alzheimer's and Related Disorders Association provides support and services such as material, support groups, financial aid for adult day care, and in-home care. The purpose of this organization is two-fold: 1) to raise money for research; and 2) to provide support to victims and families.

The American Heart Association provides similar services as those mentioned above. It too is designed to raise money for research and provide assistance to victims.

The American Lung Association is similar to those already mentioned. Each has a particular area of interest and a mission to change the dreadful effects of a particular disease.

The Diabetes Association is much like those above. These agencies are all listed in the telephone book under "services" or "associations."

It is to your advantage to gather together as much resource information as possible so as to be better prepared to meet the needs of the congregation. Most cities have a mayor's commission on aging or other such commissions that can be of great assistance to you. Call for information and volunteer to sit on the commission!

Ministry to and with the Elderly

Chapter Twelve
Biblical Directions

In a study such as this, where we have talked about ministry to and with the elderly, it is important that we ask ourselves why we should provide a ministry to the elderly. Why is this an important thing for us to do? I suppose the answer in some ways is similar to the answer to why we minister to anyone. For me, that answer is easy. We provide ministry to others out of love. And we love because we were and are loved.

The basis of my personal belief about why we love one another stems from a text in Genesis where God has just about completed creation. After each creation, God saw that it was good and moved on to create another thing. The heavens and the earth, light, heaven, dry land, sun, moon, stars, creatures of the sea, and creatures of the land were all good. When God finally created humankind, the assessment in chapter one verse 31 was that it was very good. We are a part of creation with which God was pleased. From this creation story, I have come to believe that all humanity is worthy, is acceptable, because we are created by God, and God thought that creation was very good. The second creation story talks about sin and the fall from grace, but in the first one, God is pleased.

There are numerous other Old Testament verses that talk about the responsibility of the family in caring for the elders. The fifth commandment tells us to honor our fathers and mothers. It seems clear that the aim of this commandment is to secure support for the aging parents from their children. In Old Testament times, families lived together in large groups. When the aging parents could no longer work, they did not have a Social Security system or a retirement plan. They were entirely dependent upon their children to support them economically. The way one could bring honor to his parents was by taking care of him or her when they could no longer take care of themselves.

As I recall, the Hebrew word for honor comes from a root word that means heavy or weighty. To honor a parent then means to give some weight to, or to acknowledge the importance of, the parent. This interpretation takes us away from the realm of simple obedience into the realm of personal service including the meeting of needs. Grown Hebrew children, and especially the sons, knew that their responsibility was not simply to say, "Yes, Father." They knew that they were to care for their parents just as their parents had a generation before.

Leviticus 19:32 seems to equate the honor due to parents with the honor due to God. It says, "You shall rise up before the hoary head, and honor the face of an old man, and you shall fear your God: I am the Lord." Honor toward the elderly and honor toward God are seen as parallel. It is important to note this place of honor was given to nothing else in the Old Testament. The basis of Hebrew society was around love of God and family.

The New Testament offers a few scripture verses that I believe give us some direction regarding loving and expressing our love through ministry. Mark 12:28-34 presents an important teaching of Jesus about the nature of love and the role it plays in our lives. You may recall that Jesus is responding to a question about the greatest commandment by quoting two popular Old Testament texts. The first has to do with loving God and the second deals with loving neighbors. It is commonly believed that we are unable to love another unless we feel positively toward ourselves. It seems to be human nature to value ourselves, and by telling his questioners that they should love their neighbors as themselves, Jesus was saying that love for a neighbor should be automatic, not calculated, weighed, and thoroughly debated.

Love of others is important not only for the person doing the loving, but also for the person who receives the love. In the case of the elderly, a lack of being loved has the potential for beginning a vicious cycle. If older people were not made to feel unloved, useless, unwanted, and resented, they would be less insecure, demanding, or fearful about where they fit in society. Unfortunately, our current society has decided that the elderly have little or nothing to contribute, and for some reason, the elderly have adopted that expectation.

Not being loved and valued can lead the elderly to a loss of self-esteem that is so necessary for all of us to function in a healthy manner. When the older person attempts to regain this self-esteem, they may use some less than desirable means. One way is to turn inward and to be concerned only about themselves. When the older person does this, it only feeds the negative impressions society has of them. The cycle continues.

It is the loving, compassionate grandma or grandpa who inspires us to get beyond the stereotypes and offer love to other older people. Their love, the love of God, and our love for ourselves enable us to minister to the elderly.

Jesus, as he hung dying on the cross, asked John to assume his responsibility to his mother when he said, in John 19:26, "Woman, behold your son!" and in verse 27, "Behold your mother!" The verse concludes, "... and from that hour the disciple took her to his own house." Family responsibility was simply a given.

Responsibility for older adults was seen by the early church to be important. You may recall in the book of Acts that a decision was made in chapter 6 to choose seven good men full of the Spirit and wisdom to administer the money and food that was collected to meet the needs of the widows. There were widows with no source of income who were believers. The church gave these people assistance. Many of them had themselves no doubt given all they had to the common good.

This example, one of the first administrative decisions of the church, gives us direction today to care for each other, to support one another in our time of need. And so churches from all Christian denominations have means to care for their senior citizens. It is something we are compelled to do out of love for one another.

Another text that can give us some understanding of why we minister to others is 1 Corinthians 12. You know this as the chapter where Paul is talking about the body and how all the parts of the body are important to make the body function properly. Many of the teachings found in the Bible are centered on community. Families were very important. Neighbors were important. The emphasis on the care of the elderly within the community can be found throughout the Bible. The elders were very important members of Israeli society. Given that the family was at the center of the larger community, the emphasis on the care of the elderly parents indicates that the Israelis believed that God meant for the older person not only to remain within the community, but also to receive its benefits, just as they had worked so hard to provide benefits to those who were their elders.

Looking at the text from Corinthians, it is easy to see that if Christians relate to one another as members of a body, then injury or suffering to one member has an effect on all the others. And the weaker parts should be supported by the stronger. The body of Christ has many parts. Yet this body, heterogeneous in many ways, is a unity of believers, serving God and one another. Jesus has connected every believer with himself in such a way that he lives in the believers, and they in him. This union demands that we care for one another and enables us to do just that. Not all of us are caregivers. Not all are nurses or doctors, but we can support these ministries using whatever gifts or talents we possess.

It seems clear that the biblical understanding of ministry to the elderly is based on love of neighbor and valuing the neighbor as an important part of the body. Paul gives some additional advice in Romans that I would like you to consider. Romans 3:22-24 says, "For there is no distinction; since all have sinned and fall short of the glory of God, they are justified by his grace as a gift, through the redemption which is in

Christ Jesus." My point here is simply that no one, no matter how strong or intelligent or talented, has any claim of superiority over anyone else.

The command to love one's neighbor as oneself lies at the heart of the Christian story. It is clear that none of us is better than the other and that some of us need support as we continue through life. We are all responsible for the love and care and for the ministry to the elderly in our community, in our congregation, in our family. Those who are able to provide care should do so. Other members of the body can support them while they perform services more suitable to their unique gifts.

Conclusion

Ministry to the elderly has been my calling and my ministry for many years. I know, however, that not everyone feels the same. For some, pastoral ministry of any kind is difficult. Thank God that not all people who have been called to ministry are the same as me. Who would do youth work? Nonetheless, if you are the pastor of a church, it is your responsibility to minister to the elderly. I hope that the preceding chapters have been helpful. I have attempted to provide you with some information about the physical changes the older church member will go through. In like manner, I have explained some of the neurological changes that some elderly people endure. I have showed that emotional losses are prevalent beginning with retirement and going through the many physical and emotional losses that are possible for the elderly. I am hopeful that the programs I have suggested will serve as a springboard for many others that your own church will offer to the elderly. My suggestions regarding architecture will be helpful if you plan to be building a new facility in the near future, but if not, at least I am hopeful that they have given you pause as you plan your worship and meetings.

Ministry with the elderly is harder to do than ministry to the elderly. It requires thought and planning. It also requires that we get out of the societal mindset that says once you retire you are no longer able to be effective. People prior to retirement were involved in ministry in a number of ways. Just because one ages does not mean they are ineffective. Consider the many suggestions I've offered regarding enabling the elderly to continue to be in ministry with others. You may be able to think of many others. I am sure that you know your congregation, its needs, and the abilities of your members. I simply would encourage you to allow the elderly to continue to minister to the congregation and to you.

Bibliography

Anderson, Kenneth, and Herbert Anderson. *All Our Losses, All Our Griefs.* Philadelphia, 1983.

Erikson, Erik. *Identity Youth and Crisis.* New York, 1968.

Fowler, James. *Stages of Faith: The Psychology of Human Development and the Quest for Meaning.* San Francisco, 1981.

Gelles, Jeff. "Long-Term Care Insurance Is Best Bet For Some But It's Costly." *Virginian-Pilot,* July 27, 1998, D4.

Gentzler, Richard H., Jr. *1999 International of Older Persons.* The United Methodist Committee on Older Adult Ministries, 1998.

———. "Getting Old." *Scientific America* (1973): 44-53.

Grolier Multimedia Encyclopedia (1998), s.v. "Cardiovascular."

Hooyman, Nancy R., and Wendy Lustbader. *Taking Care of Your Aging Family Members.* New York, 1996.

Kane, R. L., J. G. Ouslander, and I. B. Abrass. *Essentials of Clinical Geriatrics*, 2nd ed. New York, 1989.

Paffenbarger, R. S., A. L. Wing, and C. Hsieh. "Physical Activity, All-Cause Mortality, and Longevity of College Alumni." *New England Journal of Medicine* (314): 605

McConnell, Malcolm. "Faith Can Help You Heal." *Reader's Digest* (October 1998): 109.

U.S. Census Bureau

About The Author

Rev. Farabaugh offers a unique view of ministry to and with the elderly based on his unique career as a United Methodist minister serving local churches for fourteen years and as an administrator of various long-term care facilities for another sixteen. His insight gained from working in both of these areas is obvious in numerous examples and suggestions. He has served as a preacher, teacher, workshop leader, and a consultant over the years in an effort to help pastors and churches better understand the elderly and how to better minister to their needs.